The LMS Duchesses

THE LMS
DUCHESSES

EDITED BY
Douglas Doherty

MODEL AND ALLIED PUBLICATIONS LIMITED
13-35 Bridge Street, Hemel Hempstead, Herts,
ENGLAND

Model and Allied Publications Ltd.,
Book Division,
Station Road,
Kings Langley,
Hertfordshire, England.

First Published 1973

© Douglas Doherty 1973

ISBN 0 85242 325 X

Filmset and printed in England by
Page Bros (Norwich) Ltd,
Norwich, Norfolk.

Bound in England by
The Pitman Press,
Bath, Somerset.

Contents

Locomotives Illustrated

Acknowledgements

Acknowledgement is made to the following sources for information—
The Railway Gazette, The Railway Magazine, Stanier Locomotives by Brian Haresnape and *The Last Steam Locomotives of British Railways* by P. Ransome Wallis.

Acknowledgement is also due to the Public Relations Officer of British Rail's Midland Region for the selection of official photographs he made available for use in this book.

Introduction

No claim is made to finality of the story of the LMS 'Duchesses' with this book. The objective is to bring pleasure to the reader by seeking to re-create certain of the life and times of these locomotives via words, drawings and pictures. The qualifications of the contributors are ideally suited to just such a task.

E. A. Langridge was one of D. Drummond's last apprentices, entering Eastleigh C.M.E. Works in September 1912. After a period in the Drawing Office there under T. S. Finlayson, he joined the MR Loco. Drawing Office at Derby in 1920.

In 1945 he was put in charge of the LMS Loco. Development Office under T. F. Coleman and dealt with the last steam and diesel locos of H. G. Ivatt; the preliminary design of the Railway Executive (1947) steam locos; the British Transport Commission (1951) Sulzer-engined diesels and various railcars.

In 1954, he became Diesel Traction Assistant to the LM Regional M. & E.E. and in 1956 was appointed to the Development Unit of the BR Mechanical and Electrical Engineers. He retired in 1959, having served under 11 C.M.E's. His presentation was made by J. J. Finlayson, nephew of the man who had started him off 40 years earlier.

John Powell commenced his railway career with a mechanical apprenticeship at Derby locomotive Works. After Army service during the war, Mr. Powell held various technical appointments in the C.M. & E.E. Dept. Derby, involving close liaison with the Motive Power Dept.

Various appointments followed. Maintenance Assistant, Central Division in 1955, Assistant D.M.P.S., Newton Heath in 1957 and Motive Power Assistant, Manchester Division in 1958.

In 1958 he forsook Motive Power to become Assistant to the Divisional Manager, Edinburgh. Then became District Traffic Superintendent, Aberdeen, in 1962, and then to Scottish Region H.Q. in 1964 as Projects Officer responsible for the introduction of Freightliner and merry-go-round coal operations in Scotland. Transferred to Freightliners Ltd. from January 1st 1969 as Traffic Officer for the Scottish Area.

Mr. Powell is now Planning Officer (Operations) in the Channel Tunnel Organisation of British Railways Board.

W. A. Tuplin is too well known as an engineer, author and lifelong student of the locomotive to require further introduction.

Driver Johnson started his career in June 1944 as a cleaner at Wellington, Shropshire, on the GWR. Upon promotion to Fireman in October 1944 he was transferred to Gresty Lane, Crewe, where he fired on most classes of GWR engines with the exception of the small 2-6-2T, 47xx class 2-8-0, 10xx 'County' class and the 'Kings'.

In 1952 he transferred 'fireman to fireman' to Crewe North and was placed in No. 6 link, subsequently passing through all the links at the North Shed, and eventually spent his remaining firing years at Crewe South. He 'passed out' as a Driver in May 1957 and became registered Driver in 1961.

Since the scrapping of the steam locomotives, Driver Johnson now drives diesel and electric locomotives. A native of Crewe (and proud of it) he is known to his peers as 'Piccolo Pete'.

May 1971   Douglas Doherty
                                                           MITO, AMIMI, AMBIM

The LMS Duchesses—
their design and construction

by E. A. LANGRIDGE, F.I.Mech.E.

The design for the LMS Duchess class 4–6–2's was formulated in the Derby Loco. Drawing Office but the detail drawings were prepared partly there and partly in the Crewe Loco. D.O. The set-up at that time (1936) was—T. F. Coleman. Chief Technical Assistant at Derby in charge of Loco. and Carriage & Wagon Drawing Offices, and also with technical supervision of C.M.E. drawing offices attached to the regions. These were under day-to-day surveillance of the Mechanical Engineers of the regions concerned and normally were engaged on their own regional locomotive and plant alterations, etc. Perhaps I should also add that the Chief Loco-Draughtsmen at Derby and Crewe, at this time, were D. W. Sanford and G. R. Nicholson respectively.

A little history of the earlier LMS 4–6–2's must be recalled in order to make the picture clear at the time of the inception of the 'Duchess' design.

The boilers on Nos 6200 and 6201 had tubes 20 ft 9 in. long—reminiscent of Vincent Raven and the old NER—and 16 flue tubes each carrying two individual flow-and-return superheater elements, i.e. the steam made one pass down and back to the header. This design had been detailed from a Euston engine diagram by J. L. Francis, affectionately known by his colleagues at Derby as 'The Sailor', from his tales of his wartime service in the engine room of merchantmen with ¼ in. plate between him and the ocean. He and others had been transferred to the Derby office when it was moved from the top floor 'Under the Clock' to a former Stores building—an almost Victorian-era factory-like place. Jack (Francis) had always travelled daily to and from Crewe and secured his return to that office about 1933. He had been responsible there for the very successful Claughton Scheme 3 boiler—also used on the Baby Scots—and during his early years at Derby I worked on the next board to him, sharing a copy of the *Railway Engineer* of July 1919 containing an article on GWR boiler details, while he did the Princess boiler and I, the 5X taper. In between times we talked 'Music', for Jack was a tip-top pianist.

Thus it came about that, when the makers of the turbine, Metro-Vickers, asked for a higher superheat on the boiler for No 6202, the 'Turbomotive', it fell to my lot to detail this boiler. The overall dimensions were to be the same as those for the 'Princess', but I obtained agreement to important alterations which made it the prototype for future LMS and BR 4–6–2 designs.

In the first place the ratio of large to small tubes was altered. Using the same superheater header as before and its 32 flange connections to the 16 elements, I now put in 32 flue tubes each housing one element making a double pass for the steam in its flow and return. There were 112 small tubes. This was not, of course, the highest possible superheating arrangement, but it was feared that evaporation might suffer if more flue tubes were used.

Subsequently 6202 had a boiler of the same shape with 40 flues and is recorded as giving a temperature of 690°F in the steam chest.

A more important change from 'Princess' design was in the firebox front end shape.

It is well known that GWR designers had always advocated vertical tubeplates: on this new boiler for No 6202 and in all subsequent 4–6–2 boilers this prejudice was overcome and 'a combustion chamber', so-called, introduced. The amount of front tubeplate slope possible was determined by the hydraulic press dimensions at Crewe, where steel flanged plates were formed. Copper flanged plates were brought from manufacturers outside, ready made to shape. It was found possible, after allowing for the depth of the shaping blocks themselves, to press a plate to approximately 3 ft 0 in. depth in the finished article as shown in Fold-out at p. 18. It thus became possible to reduce the tube lengths to a more manageable figure of 19 ft 3 in. (from the original 20 ft 9 in.) and what is of greater value, to increase the firebox volume and its surface subject to radiant heat from the firegrate.

What has made this and subsequent LMS 4–6–2 fireboxes unique is the way in which the semi-cylindrical shape of the throat plate at the boiler barrel end is 'faded out' gradually to suit the flat face at the foundation ring. Normally, when a cylindrical barrel runs into a sloping throat plate one gets a 'hump' on each side, right and left, in the firebox, whereas, in the design under discussion, the radius is specified to be 'constantly changing from that at the barrel end to the flat at the foundation ring'. It is very difficult to get this shape across to the reader's mind without a model: and it was equally difficult for the pattern-maker constructing the press blocks. The draughtsman—myself—had more or less to spoke-

1

Four transverse views of a "Duchess" in streamlined cladding. See fold out at p. 18 for cross sectional side elevation and plan of a "Duchess".

Cross section through smokebox.   Front view.

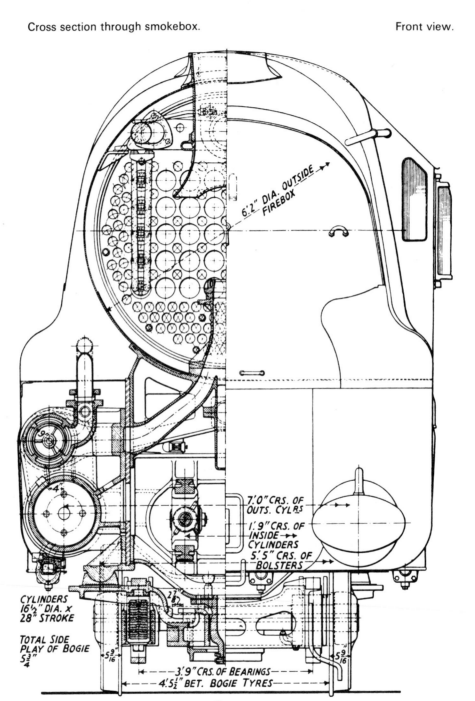

6'.2" DIA. OUTSIDE FIREBOX

7'.0" CRS. OF OUTS. CYLRS

1'. 9" CRS. OF INSIDE CYLINDERS

5'. 5" CRS. OF BOLSTERS

CYLINDERS 16½" DIA. X 28" STROKE

TOTAL SIDE PLAY OF BOGIE 5¾"

3'. 9" CRS. OF BEARINGS

4'.5½" BET. BOGIE TYRES

2

Cross section through firebox.   Cross section through boiler.

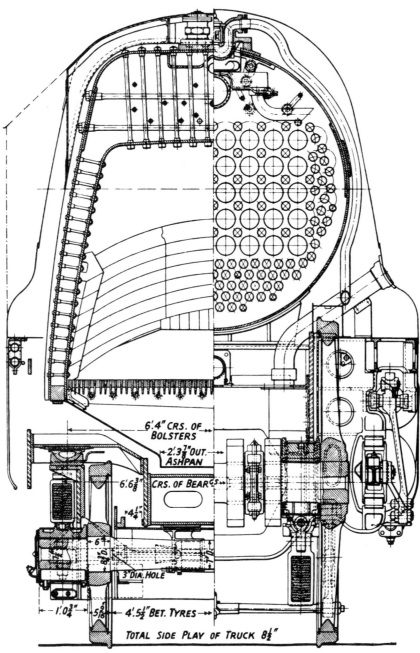

6'.4" CRS. OF BOLSTERS

2'.3⅞" OUT. ASHPAN

6'.6⅜" CRS. OF BEAR⁀ˢ

4¼"

6½"

8¼"D.

3" DIA. HOLE

1'.0¾"

5⁹⁄₁₆"

4'.5½" BET. TYRES

TOTAL SIDE PLAY OF TRUCK 8½"

Leading dimensions and weights

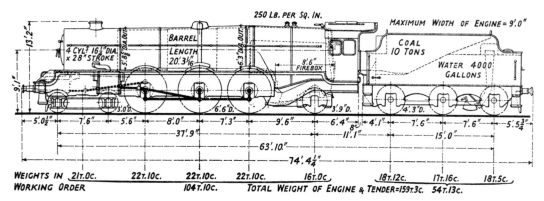

Princess Royal Class.

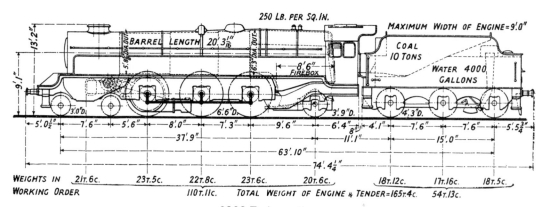

6202 Turbomotive.

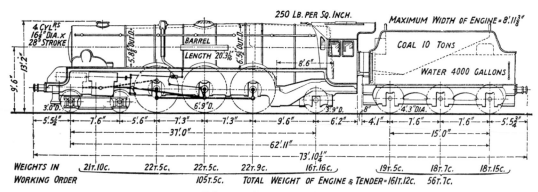

Princess Coronation Class.

shave off the 'humps' on the pattern maker's first effort; but after I had demonstrated what was in my mind, no difficulty occurred subsequently.

The Crewe boiler shop was praised generally by Stanier for its work, although he was critical of some of its tools in his early days on the LMS. Very reasonably, he had no time for their 3-roller tube expanders and brought in a 6-roller type to avoid the tendency of the former to make triangular holes. He also disliked the $1\frac{1}{16}$ in. rivets used in the 'Royal Scot' boilers: the pressure used on the hydraulic rivetter in closing these distorted the edges of the lap joint plates. All the boilers during his time on the LMS had $\frac{7}{8}$ in. rivets in $\frac{15}{16}$ in. holes. On the other hand, Fell, the boiler shop foreman surprised Stanier by saying that Crewe could drill the wrapper plates for the 4–6–2 boiler in one piece on the flat and before rolling to shape, whereas Swindon had always made them in three pieces with a joint strap on the water line, even on their 4–6–0 boilers. The craftsmanship in the Pattern and Boiler shops at Crewe was obviously of a high order. The 'limits and fits' for stays and rivets worked to in the boiler shop were to the best machine shop practice.

Another tricky job due to this throat plate design came up in marking out the stay holes on a constantly curving surface. These stays, like all others in the water spaces, are required to be at right angles to the copper plate in order to obtain a good seating for the protecting nut, where these are used, and to obtain full screw threads in the copper plate and a good head, in the case of copper or alloy stays, riveted over. The stays in this throat plate were made of monel metal and had heads riveted over: the only way of obtaining a satisfactory pitching of these on the copper plate was to do the

scribing out on the first firebox. From this a flexible template was made and this was used for marking out subsequent fireboxes. It was also awkward for fitting of the fire-brick arch. Normally, this butts up against the flat surface of the tubeplate or throat plate: in this case it had to be built up against a constantly changing curved surface. The waist of the firebox was also wider, due to the combined curves, at the point of crossing of the engine main frames. These required some shaping at the top edge to clear the firebox plate.

Before leaving this prototype design, it should be pointed out that no thinning down or scarfing of steel plates was required except at the lap joint with the foundation ring. The way in which the steel wrapper laps over the Belpaire corner plate and the abutting throat plate, which, in their turn both lap over the boiler barrel plate can be seen from the drawing. Finally, this design produced a useful saving in weight as almost 1 ft 6 in. length of barrel, tubes and water was eliminated.

Having explained the general advance towards the 'Duchess' boiler, let us look at the situation in 1935: in various countries locos were being designed with a view to high-speed trains, e.g. Wagner in Germany and Chapelon in France. At home, Gresely had produced *Silver Link*: the LMS had only 13 4–6–2's by the end of 1935. It was then that E402 was issued to cover the building of 5 more 'Princesses Nos 6213–6217.

Nevertheless, Coleman and one of his senior men at Derby, had been working for sometime on various schemes for a 'bigger and better design' than the Princess. The reader may very well ask, Why? From the designer's point of view, I can only reply that there is always the urge to improve. The true designer wants to be kept busy: like any other artist he

improves with practice. To achieve a change, broadly the old requirements of having 'the right men in the right position at the right time' applies. And in the early '30s there seemed to be the urge everywhere to try and advance rail transportation. Apart from detail troubles that could be put right fairly easily: on paper, to the discriminating eye, the 'Princess' design did not seem to be using material to the best advantage. There were the four valve gears, the spread out wheelbase, and the boiler seemed to be a long drawn out affair. From technical magazines, etc., one could see what was happening elsewhere and felt that one could do as well, or better than the others. On the commercial side, there was always the publicity value of having 'something new this season'. No doubt the publicity man is apt to be 'the tail that wags the dog' at times and the engineer has to swallow such things as streamlining and smoothing which, in his view, are neither beautiful or useful: even in later years the design consultant, so called, had the Diesel Shunter access doors smoothed over with the result that the examining fitter could not find the handles on a dark night, and neither would the doors themselves fold back. In achievement little could be finer than the demonstration runs with No 6201 on the Euston–Glasgow and return runs: yet the thought that the design could be improved persisted and Coleman convinced the 'powers that be'. Undoubtedly every new design is a gamble and perhaps we were luckier than Chambers had been. In his young days, Coleman had played football for Stoke-on-Trent and perhaps he knew better when to shoot for goal.

The main idea was to use a larger diameter driving wheel, 6 ft 9 in. being the next standard tyre size, with the largest size boiler barrel possible. By sacrificing the

Top Left Camden M.P.D. 25/8/59. On the turntable after having brought the up 'The Caledonian' into Euston is 46242 *City of Glasgow*. Waiting patiently for her turn is 46204 *Princess Louise,* one of the original Stanier Pacifics.
Photo by Douglas Doherty.

Bottom Left Coming off Crewe North M.P.D. is 'Princess Royal' class No 46210 *Lady Patricia* to await arrival of the train it will take forward to Euston. 4/8/58.
This is one of the batch of original Stanier Pacifics from which the 'Duchesses' were derived.
Photo by Douglas Doherty.

Below One of the original batch of Stanier Pacifics, No 6201 *Princess Elizabeth,* now happily preserved in running order. This first series consisted of twelve engines, Nos 6200/1, 6203–12. The odd one out was No 6202, the Turbomotive 4–6–2. The official class designation was 'Princess Royal' class.
Photo by London Midland Region (B.R.)

standard GW figure of 2 ft 0 in. hitherto used on Stanier boilers, between the inner and outer top firebox plates, and also their standard radius on the Belpaire steel firebox wrapper plate in cross-section, it was possible to obtain a 6 ft $5\frac{1}{2}$ in. maximum diameter barrel, keeping within the loading gauge corners. At the same time two alternative arrangements for cylinders and valve gear were drawn out. Scheme 'A' had the GWR (or if you prefer it—the Princess style), i.e. outside cylinders over the rear bogie wheel and the inside ones over the leading bogie wheel centre-line with a rocking lever *forward* of the outside steam chest and rear of the inside steam chest. Scheme 'B' had the inside cylinders forward of the bogie centre-line and the outside ones to its rear, with the rocking lever to the inside valve gear at the *back* of the outside cylinders. We all knew the arrangement of the 4 cylinders on the LNW Claughtons in which the rocking levers were placed forward with valve spindle crossheads sliding on the lever ends to take care of the versed sine movement. I, myself, had worked on Drummond's LSWR 4-cyl. 4–6–0's, where he advanced from the staggered pitching of outside and inside cylinders (as on GW engines) on his 330 class and old 453 class to his 4-cylinder in-line arrangement on his last 443's, later known as 'Paddleboxes'. By doing so, he got rid of the racking forces which loosen cylinders and stretchers and which, in every example from that day to the 'Kings' and 'Princesses', has taken place with the staggered arrangement. The Drummond arrangement of driving the rocking levers, placed behind the cylinders, involved a die-block, pinned in the outside valve spindle and sliding in a rectangular slot in the end of the rocking lever as shown in the fold-out at p. 19. This was not

much better than the Claughton design which really dated back to Webb's 'Alfred the Greats': they were all too full of sliding surfaces. Coleman, from his earlier position at Horwich, was familiar with the Hughes 4-cyl. 4–6–0 arrangement where the rocking lever is driven by a short link having pin joints, one to the outside valve spindle extension and one to the rocker. This latter arrangement was shown on Scheme 'B'. In order to keep the outside connecting rod down to 11 ft 0 in. centres the spacing between the 1st and 2nd coupled wheels had to be reduced from 8 ft 0 in. on the 'Princesses' to 7 ft 3 in. This made the loco. more compact, but did away with the equal length connecting rods and identical valve events which were made a feature of by those who prepared the original 'Princess' layout.

Scheme 'B' seemed too revolutionary to be accepted at H.Q., but the unexpected happened. When Coleman went up to Euston with the two schemes to see Stanier a few days before his departure for India, Stanier agreed to Scheme 'B' and said that five locos. must be ready for the 1937 $6\frac{1}{2}$-hour London and Glasgow service.

Things then moved rapidly: the material sheets and drawings already issued for Nos 6213–6217 were cancelled where necessary, and order E402 became Engines 6220–6224, thus avoiding the fateful '13'.

In any new design, an engine diagram showing weights and wheel spacing is prepared and also an end view giving throw-overs on a curve regarded as standard by the C.E. and usually 6 or 7 chains. This has to be agreed to by the C.E., for he is the one Chief Officer at whose bidding trains may be stopped from running without question. The weight estimate is usually made in the D.O. by considering the differences between the new design and a

'pattern loco.' It is thus imperative that the true weights of the 'pattern loco' are known, otherwise the estimates for the new design may be sadly incorrect. An instance of what can happen took place in connection with the LMS (Parallel boiler) 2–6–4 Tank. The estimated weights for this design were based on the book weight of the MR 0–6–4 Tank built in Deeley's time. Unfortunately an actual weighing of this engine was not made at the time the 2–6–4 design was being schemed out and the latter came out at least 4 tons heavier than estimate. This was due to the fact that the diagram weight of the

In the case of E402 we were more fortunate: we had actual weights of No 6200, viz. 111 tons 18 cwt. After thinning down castings, etc., No 6201 came out at 108 tons. It was evident that E402 could be kept down to the estimate of 106 tons without much difficulty.

For the diagram showing the end view of loco. in the loading gauge and the points of fouling, a plan of the fixed (coupled) wheelbase and the bogie and pony truck centre pins is drawn out on tracing paper. This is laid on a drawing of the standard, say 6 chain, curve which usually is preserved on mounted, unshrinkable paper in the D.O. and drawn out at 3 in. = 1 ft scale. The diagram of bogie wheels and centre, and that of the pony truck wheels and pivot arm centre, are each drawn out separately to the 3 in. scale. These two diagrams are laid on the main frame diagram in the correct longitudinal positions and the necessary side movement measured off to bring the wheels within the curve. Allowance has to be made throughout for clearance of boxes in guides, etc., and for tyre clearance. On E402 the usual thick + thin + thick ARLE profiles were used on L.I.T. coupled wheels respectively, but

No 6202 Turbomotive.   *Above* View of the right hand side showing the reverse turbine casing.   *Below* View of the left hand side showing forward turbine casing.
Photos by London Midland Region (B.R.)

pony and bogie tyres had a special thick flange to increase the life before reaching scrapping size. These thick flanges also made the wheels tighter in the gauge and check rails. Taking everything into account it was found that we required $2\frac{3}{4}$ in. at front bogie centre and $4\frac{1}{4}$ in. at pony truck axle centre line, each way, i.e. right and left. Most civil engineers will allow some infringement of the loading gauge on curves provided that this is above station platform level. This gives the designer some freedom at cylinders and steam chests where width is valuable.

Civil engineers vary in their outlook: the old MR loco. designer was particularly handicapped. In that office it was the practice to draw out, for their own information, a Bending Moment Diagram due to the proposed loco. weights on the track and from this to derive an Equivalently Uniformly Distributed Load Curve for various bridge spans. This they compared with the 'Worthington 1911 Curve' which had been given them by the Civil Engineer of that name. Tender weights were also included, of course. In actual fact, this curve limited the development of loco. size on the MR and even more so, as Worthington objected to wheel spacings closer than 8 ft 0 in. + 8 ft 6 in. The catalogue of parts that had to be removed, in MR days, from the S.D. 2–8–0 and the MR 0–10–0 Banker to enable them to be moved from the works at Derby to their areas of operation read quite fantastically. With the advent of E. F. C. Trench (of the LNWR) as Civil Engineer of the LMS things eased up considerably.

As I have already stated, for E402 the detail design and drawing was shared between Derby and Crewe D.O.'s. By this date both offices had become fairly cosmopolitan, for besides including some of the old MR and LNWR men they had each collected some ex-Contract Shop men. Also former

Above Right The first of the 'Duchesses' No 6220 *Coronation* in blue livery with silver bands. This second series of Stanier Pacifics had Nos 6220–6257. Actually the last engine built never ran as an LMS engine and carried the No 46257 from first being built, this being the British Railways number. From 1948, 40,000 was added to each 'Duchess' class running number. The official class designation was 'Princess Coronation' class. The description 'Duchesses' applied to the class was unofficial and had its origins in lay enthusiast circles.
Photo by London Midland Region (B.R.)

Middle Right In original blue livery and silver bands throughout. The LMS 'Coronation Scot' express approaching Oxenholme, headed by No 6220 *Coronation.*
Photo by F. R. Hebron.

Below Right No 6227 *Duchess of Devonshire* in grey livery, crimson lake and yellow band style.
Photo by London Midland Region (B.R.)

Horwich, Stoke, St. Rollox, and men originating from Ashford and Eastleigh.

The work of detailing the boiler and other parts above the platform was allocated to Crewe and the remainder to Derby. The boiler design as a whole depends on the maximum barrel diameter at the throat plate end. All Stanier period boilers up to this date, as already stated, had preserved the 2 ft spacing of inner and outer firebox roof plates. In the present design agreement had been reached to reduce this to 1 ft 10 in. allowing the inner firebox roof to be lifted 2 in. and so giving more area to the tubeplate for tubes. As will be seen from the boiler and firebox drawings the water space is carried up from the foundation ring forming an annular space between the steel and copper throat plates. Thus the overall sizes of the firebox tubeplate in all directions are determined. The pitching of the tubes in the plate is governed by the following considerations.

Flue tubes are normally supplied by the manufacturers at $5\frac{1}{8}$ in.

nominal dia. x 7 S.W.G. Small tubes are available in many sizes and the one selected by the designer usually bears a ratio of length to diameter of about 100 to 1. The basis of this ratio is the fact that resistance to gas flow down a tube is related to its mean hydraulic depth. D. W. Sanford restated this in terms of Area/Surface or A/S ratios and also suggested a Resistance Criterion factor for the comparison of boiler performance. Sanford had a remarkably clear, logical brain (he was a 1st Cl. Hons. in Maths. Cantab. man) and a gift for giving simple explanations of any abstruse problems. However, he suffered, like others who cannot suffer lesser brains gladly. During the period after the 1914/18 war, he was virtually the secretary of the A.R.L.E. when Sir Henry Fowler was in power there. Heat transfer increases with gas speed and surfaces exposed to radiant heat are worth their weight in gold. Thus the small tube size selected was $2\frac{3}{8}$ in. o.d. x11 S.W.G. Each flue tube carried a triple element, i.e. six cross-sections, 1 in. o.d. x11

Above A batch of 'Duchesses', Nos 6230–4, appeared in 1938 in the non-streamlined form shown here. The livery is grey, LMS pre-war style.
Photo by London Midland Region (B.R.)

Top Right Train end view of streamlined tender.
Photo by W. Potter.

Bottom Right Locomotive end view of streamlined tender.
Photo by W. Potter.

S.W.G. the steam making one pass, out and return. The elements finished about 1 ft short of the firebox for the longest and 2 ft 6 in. for the shortest return bend. The *A/S* for flues was about 1/550, for the tubes 1/430. This gives some idea of the proportion of gas passing down each kind of tube. The superheat temperature will bear some relation to these ratios and also to the characteristics of the elements themselves. The search for increasing the amount of super-heat went on until the last days of the steam loco. design. Various types of element were made by the Superheater Company either to their own ideas or to those of their customers. A few non-Schmidt types were the 'Sinu-flow' having depressions to sine curve shapes along the tube: the 5P4 type: the bifurcated types one of which had the return pipe (a single large

diameter) lagged at the smokebox end to prevent heat loss. In the present case the triple element was used.

The pitching of the tubes was then schemed out: the ruling being that the 'bridges' must not be less than $\frac{3}{4}$ in., the tube hole was $\frac{1}{8}$ in. less than the tube nominal size, the tube itself being swaged down before insertion, a practice not allowed in GWR boilers. Another break-away was in allowing the flue tubes to be more closely pitched at the firebox end than at the smokebox end, entailing the inclination of tapped holes for these in the firebox tubeplate. In setting out the tubes, care is always taken to keep the holes away from the plate corner radii and it sometimes happens, as in the present case, that a row of small tubes at the top of the tube-plate is more valuable in using the

area economically than in pushing the flue tubes themselves to the top. The scheme adopted in the E402 boiler had 129 tubes at $2\frac{3}{8}$ in. o.d. and 40 flues at $5\frac{1}{8}$ in. o.d. (nominal). The free areas were:

Through flue tubes	3·66 sq. ft
Through small tubes	3·23 sq. ft
Total Free Area	6·89 sq. ft

This free area is only 13·8% of the grate area, showing how diffi-cult it is to get a high percentage, within the British loading gauge, for an engine with a large grate.

The diameter of the boiler barrel at the front end is dependant on the pitching of the tubes adopted. The LMS figure transversely for flue tubes is $6\frac{1}{4}$ in. This is to accommodate element fixing flanges on the superheated header. Vertically the dimension is reduced to 6 in. The small tubes are pitched as at the firebox tubeplate, room

for about half-a-dozen washout plugs is required plus a reasonable distance from the flange radius of the drumhead tubeplate. Although it is not disastrous if the tube bank is so high at the smokebox end that it becomes uncovered by the water on steep inclines or surges, it is felt it is inadvisable to run the tubes much higher than their firebox level. The Drawing Office in its scheme had already pointed out the advantages of the truly conical boiler barrel in regard to easy machining and assembly as compared with the previous GW pattern in which the taper barrel has its bottom plates level; and the true cone arrangement was agreed to. The minimum diameter at the front end of barrel was thus fixed at 5 ft $8\frac{5}{8}$ in.

The specified working pressure was 250 lb. per sq. in., and the minimum factor of safety 4·75. Boiler steel plate material, 2% nickel steel. The design of boiler joints using $\frac{7}{8}$ rivets in $\frac{15}{16}$ in. holes was normal, i.e. double riveted with an extra reinforcing row through inside strap and barrel on the longitudinal seams. The usual longitudinal stays slung from the barrel supported the flat portion of the tube plate.

Coming to the design of the firebox, the overall dimensions at the cab end are settled from a consideration of the height of fittings to be fixed within the loading gauge, e.g. safety valves: space for lookout from cab forward between boiler clothing and cabside plates: depth of ashpan required and position of main frames. Thus the slope of the roof plates can be fixed bearing in mind that they are to be curved to the usual 18 ft radius for inside and 19 ft 10 in. radius for outside plates. The slope of the firebox sides requires great care in working out as the wrapper plates must have truly plane surfaces with no twists. As a curved cross-section was also specified, but at the same time, a straight

sided (although tapering overall) foundation ring was required for practical reasons, such as form of fireboxes, etc., one has of necessity to run the line of commencement of radius parallel with the slope of the roof. Above this line all cross-sections are similar, although they increase in width from back to front where the width of firebox at boiler centre matches up with the barrel diameter. Below this line the plates drop vertically to match the foundation ring face. Joining up the roof with curvature already mentioned and sides curved as described above is a 9 in. radius on the steel plate which just brings the clothed boiler within the loading gauge. The inner (copper) wrapper plate cannot stand such a large radius being a weaker material and therefore has a 5 in. radius in the corner. The radii of the door plate corners and Belpaire front corners are normal: the changing radii of the throat plates are similar to that on the prototype (No 6202) boiler already described.

The inner firebox at all times must be designed so that it can be assembled and inserted as a unit within the steel one. As design departed from the simple rectangular shape this became more of a problem. LNW and NER designs reversed the steel backplate flange. Thus, instead of dropping the inner box through the foundation ring hole, they inserted it through the backplate opening, making the closure by riveting through the exposed back plate flange and wrapper plate, instead of through the foundation ring riveting. Wide grates assist in allowing copper inner boxes to be 'angled' into position.

The staying of the copper plate to the steel in the area of the water legs is by means of $\frac{3}{4}$ in. Monel metal stays on the outside rows and by $\frac{5}{8}$ in. special steel stays for the rest of the area. The work of planning the layout of these is a work of patience by the draughts-

man concerned. The pitch is determined from the normal formulae by Napier for flat plate staying and, in the case for nutted and/or riveted stays came out at approximately 3 in.

The staying of the copper plate to the roof plate is made by steel stays, nominally $\frac{7}{8}$ in. in the body, screwed into inner and outer plates and nutted where possible; otherwise with ends riveted over. The pitching, being governed mostly by the weak copper plate, is similar to that of water space stays. Transverse steel stays, nominally 1 in. dia. tie the firebox steel sides together and are screwed into the wrapper plate which is suitably stiffened in this area by liner plates, thus giving a full thread to the stays. Longitudinal stays from the barrel support the flat steel firebox backplate.

The thickness of the firebox steel plates is decided on largely from experience rather than from strength considerations. Double riveted lap joints are used for all steel joint plates and single riveted ones for copper plate joints.

Tapered washout plugs at firebox roof level and washout doors (having lead insertion joints) are arranged at strategic points just above the foundation ring. Oval holes for washout are better than screwed-in plugs at points where much 'rodding-out' is likely to take place at washout periods. The doors being inserted from outside and seating inside the plates, are largely self-sealing.

Boiler construction is still very much of an art. The steel plates are ordered from outside to rectangular shapes. The boiler shop themselves make templates of the final shape required and of the drilling required, mostly done on the flat, so that the finished plates will conform to the dimensions of the boiler as given on the D.O. drawings. The pressed plates are formed hot under the hydraulic press. The necessary die-blocks are cast in

Above No 6240 *City of Coventry* in wartime black livery.
Photo by London Midland Region (B.R.)

Below Commencing with this engine (but in original streamline form), double chimneys and draughting arrangements were fitted to all new 'Duchesses'. No 6235 *City of Birmingham* is shown here as she emerged from Crewe Works after she had had her streamlining shorn away. All other streamlined 'Duchesses' were subsequently de-streamlined. The tapered smokeboxes were replaced by ones of normal shape eventually.

The smoke deflectors were added to all the 'Duchesses' from this engine onwards. *City of Birmingham* is in grey livery, 1946 style.
Photo by London Midland Region (B.R.)

the foundry from patterns prepared in the pattern shop. After pressing, the plate edges are sawn off to shape as necessary to form caulking edges, rivet holes, etc., marked off.

The front (drumhead) tubeplate and firebox backplate are faced up as required for the various seatings and drilled for rivet and stud fixings for these. Holes for tubes, stays, etc., are bored in the plates to jig or to drawing: stiffener plates fixed where specified. The boiler machine shop uses methods and works to limits as in the ordinary machine shop.

At an earlier date on the LMS and following a visit of J. E. Anderson to America, seatings for mountings were dispensed with. The mountings themselves had their flanges reinforced and the joint made with a conical loose ring fitting between the mounting and the chamfered hole in the boiler plate. Leakage, distorted flanges and broken studs soon 'put paid' to this practice however.

Pressings for the dome are made in the usual way. Holes for jointing plates are in some cases drilled undersize as experience in assembly has indicated. Those for the Monel metal stays in the throat plate were not drilled until the firebox had been completely put together. The foundation ring faces are machined

and drilled. The ring forging itself is normally made up by welding together sections of bar.

The rolling of the wrapper plate is done cold and in stages: the lines of the commencement of the radii are marked out on the flat plate and the position of the final boiler centre line. The bottom corners of the plate are thinned down by machining to suit the foundation ring: formerly this operation was done by heating the plate corner and hammering it. The formation of these plates to finished shape is a fine example of the boiler-maker's art.

To overcome the difficulty of getting the longitudinal edges of the barrel plates to shape on the rolls it was the practice to press the first 12 in. or so of the plate to the required shape. The plates can then be put in the rolls for obtaining the rest of the curvature, which is done cold. The machining of the plate edges, which is done before pressing and on the flat, is done on an edge planer working to a profile developed by the boiler shop to give the conical finished shape. The truly conical design of E402 boiler simplified this operation considerably from that required on previous designs and also the squaring-up operation where one barrel overlaps the adjoining one.

The barrel plates are then assembled together with drumhead tubeplate, dome, etc., held together by a few tacking bolts, checked up for alignment using lines previously scribed on the plates. The assembly is up-ended, placed on the table of the tower drilling machine and all holes drilled to finished size and cleaned out.

The steel firebox is treated similarly, but water space stay holes may not be opened out until the copper box is fitted within. Great care is taken to ensure that the top half of the throat plate (with Belpaire corners) butts up to the bottom portion of the throat to form a tight seal.

Welding up of barrel and other plates was in its infancy at this time. The LMS had got as far as repairing grooved plates by building up electrically. Sealing lengths of barrel plate joints and sealing seatings for boiler mountings was also done, thus doing away with expensive caulking and fullering operations.

Copper being an expensive commodity, it was found convenient to order the inside firebox wrapper plate to a shape approximating that of the finished plate size as developed on the flat. The copper tubeplate was ordered as a flat plate, 1 in. thick in the tube area, thinned down in the flange area to finished size. The throat plate was ordered exactly to finished shape and dimensions: the reason here is that manufacturers of copper plate have their own technique for dealing with such plates and guaranteeing uniform thickness and quality. The railway make blocks for the other plates and flange them under the hydraulic press. As with the steel plates the boiler shop prepare a jig for shaping and drilling the copper wrapper plate on the flat. The flanged plates (except the throat plate) are drilled for water space stays, rivets, etc., as shown on drawings and, after pressing, the flanges are also drilled. In addition the firebox tubeplate is bored for the flue tubes and the holes tapped and chamfered according to drawing.

The copper box plates are assembled, checked for alignment, rivet holes in joints drilled through to size. It is then inserted within the steel box and clearances at corners, sides and roof checked for agreement with drawing. Agreement between steel and copper flanges must be maintained also at firehole ring. If all is well at this final check, the holes through from the foundation ring are drilled to size, cleaned out, and the copper box withdrawn and seams riveted up. It is then assembled with the steel box, whose seams have also been riveted up, and is ready to be attached to the barrel. This will have had the supports to the frame stretchers lined up on the underside and been taken to the hydraulic riveting machine whose long vertical arms can close rivets as the boiler is slung longways from a crane.

Continuous thread in the transverse stays is ensured by using long taps although the entry end is larger in diameter than the far end in order to ease the running in of stays. Water space stays are tapped the same size in each plate and at right angles to the copper

plate in order to secure good seatings for the protecting nuts on the firebox ends. The roof stays are slightly larger diameter in the steel than in the copper but again at right angles to the latter. The end three rows of stays, here, are riveted over in the firebox in order to facilitate the insertion of half (or full) tubeplates when required in future repairs; the remainder have protecting nuts. Washers and nuts are fitted at the outside of the steel plate except on stays in the outside longitudinal rows where, due to the fact that they are within the corner radius, their heads have to be riveted over.

The foregoing touches on some of the technique of the now defunct art of locomotive boiler building.

The smokebox wrapper plate, having been drilled and cut to profile on the flat is rolled to form a cylinder with ends butting and V -welded. (In the early streamlined engines the shape was flattened towards the front.) It is passed over the distance ring on the boiler front barrel, and riveted up, the rivets passing through wrapper distance piece and boiler plate. Considerable weight was saved here by substituting a single riveted ring instead of the GWR double riveted type and also by using a wrapper plate $\frac{3}{8}$ in. instead of $\frac{1}{2}$ in. thick.

The boiler is far stronger than the frame when considered as a longitudinal beam, and the designer therefore uses it to support the frame and wheels, etc., when the loco. is being lifted. To this end, vertical connections, which may be considered as boiler supports normally (although, in lifting, they become ties), are arranged at convenient positions. At the smokebox, the wrapper is riveted to a small frame stretcher containing exhaust steam passages to blast pipe. The main front fixing is under the front barrel; a sliding support under the rear barrel; and the main rear support under

the foundation ring front end. The boiler mountings in the cab comprise two standard water gauges. The difficulty of reading the water line in these led to various types of reflector being tried. A main steam fountain with internal supply pipe from dome and under control of a main shut-down valve had individual valves controlling supply to injectors, carriage warming, brake ejector, making a cumbersome arrangement high up in the cab. Wire-wound handles of the GW type had proved too 'finicky' for LMS conditions and wheels with spokes had returned in their place. The usual centrally mounted blower valve and operating handles for the hooter were fitted. The firehole door was of the sliding type with hollow doors intended to allow access of air to fire through grids and slots in the walls. Firehole deflector plate, as usual, depended on the firehole stiffening ring for its location. The regulator handle in its shut position hung some 45° below centreline on the driver's (l.h.) side. At one time a 'drifting catch' had been fitted corresponding to a 'cracked regulator' position.

Feed water treatment had been carried out in different ways at various dates. Deeley, on the MR, with Archbutt, the chemist, had installed small plants, but later more severe softening was felt to be the answer. The standard LMS practice involved the fitting of a 'continuous blowdown valve' discharging about 7% of the boiler water consumption on to the track. Later, after very natural strong objections from engine crews, this discharge valve operated under control of the injector steam valve, with the hope that illegal stoppage of the discharge would be prevented. Towards the rear of firebox top 4 safety valves of standard LMS short type were mounted on seatings let into the firebox proper, in order to keep their tops within the loading gauge.

Left No 6252 *City of Leicester* in war time black livery, streamlined tender.

Below No 6245 *City of London,* streamlined and wartime black livery.
Photos by London Midland Region (B.R.)

The dome on the middle barrel provided access to and room for a main regulator with valves working on horizontal faces. This type had replaced the smokebox regulator of earlier Stanier designs. The slots and holes in the slides were arranged to give a curve of opening area directly proportional to the movement of the driver's regulator handle in cab. The mechanism for working the valves themselves from the rotatable regulator rod used two forked levers; one on each side of the regulator head, pinned to a shaft which had one lower lever giving a 1 to 1 ratio and connected by link to an arm on the regulator rod. The forks of the levers meshed with suitable slots in the valve slides themselves. A manhole on the top of the front barrel carried two boiler feed water clack boxes. Due to the newer water softening arrangements, the former type of so-called removeable trays was not fitted: a simple deflector arrangement directing the feed water down the barrel of the boiler.

The superheater header was a simple casting fixed to the drum-head tubeplate. It had countersunk facings to suit the superheater element flanges which were fixed by tee-headed bolts slipped into machined slotted ways in the header casting. The 7 in. dia. main internal steam pipe was expanded and ferruled into the drumhead tubeplate and secured by cone joint and bolts, in the usual way, at the regulator header casting.

The 40 flue tubes were screwed into the firebox tubeplate and fitted hard up against the chamfer on the water side. They were beaded over in the firebox after the removal of protruding screw threads and expanded at the firebox end. It was a practice in Crewe shops to provide one hole slightly larger than standard through which to pass the small tubes: these were finally expanded and beaded over in their holes at the firebox end in

the lower rows at the smokebox: others were simply expanded. Originally, Stanier boilers had tubes with a reverse taper at the firebox end, thus holding them extremely tightly at that end. The beading of small tubes in the smokebox followed a very old Crewe practice.

Saturated steam connections on the superheater header took steam to the atomiser steam valve, mounted outside the smokebox wrapper plate, and to the tube cleaner cock on the smokebox front plate—typical Stanier fittings. Steam to the blower ring, cored out and drilled as part of the blast pipe cap, came from the fitting in cab. Also in the smokebox were the two main steam pipes from the superheater header to branch tee-pieces mounted low down on the smokebox wrapper where supplies to inside and outside cylinders divided. This arrangement eliminated awkward packed glands of previous designs.

The smokebox proper is not considered to be another boiler barrel as in GW practice and is therefore of lighter construction. The door had the usual GW style of fixing: dart with tee-head working in a slot of the cross bar, the end being screwed to take the central fastening handle which provided the necessary tension. The front plate was a pressing with the flanged portion machined to 45° to match up to the door itself, which is likewise machined. An inclined strip catches a projection on the door itself, as it is being closed, lifting that end of the door so that the whole becomes central with its hole, thus easing very considerably the work involved in closing and securing this type of door. The cross bar, being a heavy forging, is pivoted at each end. Removal of one of the pins allows the bar to be swung out of the way through the door opening—a much better design than those of Drummond

where the bar had to be lifted out of brackets.

The original chimney was a normal iron casting with hollow rim. The ejector exhaust ring was bolted on to the chimney bottom. It had a cored passage and a large number of holes drilled at an angle to guide the exhaust up the chimney. This arrangement involved casting a thick ring, drilling at an angle through this and then turning down to barrel size— a rather expensive proceeding. Single chimneys were thought to be sufficiently drastic by Stanier and most engineers at that time. An experimental double chimney had been fitted to No 6201 some time earlier, but the inspector's report was non-committal and the idea faded away. There was a feeling in some quarters that economy could best be obtained by burning as little coal as possible rather than by turning out as much horse-power as possible: it depends on which side of the equation one is interested in. In the late '20s Riddles remarked one evening as I happened to be walking with others by the line-side from office to station—"There you are, Langridge! That's the thing you want, £500 a time." It was a LNWR DX or similar goods loco. going by, cheap in first cost, no doubt, but probably heavy in repairs and fuel bills—but 'economical' if you looked at it in the right way.

The blast pipe cap was a plain casting apart from having a cored passage for the blower steam exit up the chimney. The jumper cap had been abandoned on later engines of the previous build. I think it was Sanford who remarked on the poor logic of the argument in its favour, i.e. that it provided a freer exhaust; for before you could get the extra openings the exhaust itself had to lift the weight of the loose cap—about 15 lb. At one time, Swindon's sheet of blast pipe and chimney ratios were worked to: but as they brought in

Drawing showing double chimney and blastpipe.

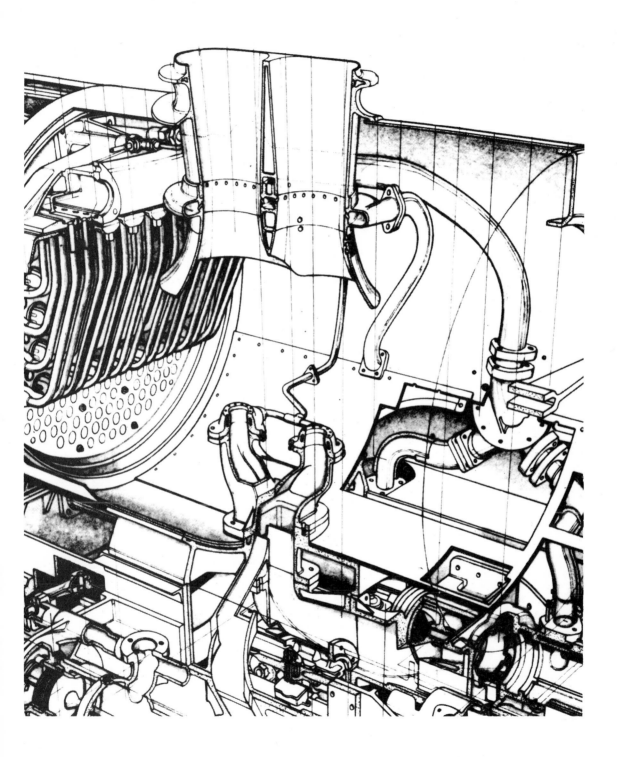

such things as heating surface figures they could only apply to Swindon characteristic designs. In the case of the locos under discussion, Coleman had his own ideas of shape of exhaust cone, etc., and put them into practice.

No spark arrester or deflector plates were fitted originally, but later a so-called 'self-cleaning' arrangement was fitted involving expanded metal sheets in frames across the smokebox with a horizontal table plate and front skirt which forced exhaust gases, etc., from tubes to pass through the mesh. This was all part of the scheme to reduce Motive Power Depot costs in ash removal and preparation time. It had not the menace of the original GW spark deflector plates where careless latching of the inclined plate could allow it to drop on the blast pipe cap and cause a 'blow-back'.

To meet the edicts of the Commercial Department a false clothing, 'streamlining' was fitted to some of the early batches of these locos; its scientific value was small. The practical disadvantages of closed-in mechanical parts, hidden sandbox and mechanical lubricator box lids and smokebox doors and the necessity of having ladders to enable cleaners to wipe down the clothing proved too much of a drawback and in due time 'streamlining' was removed from these locos. This required a great deal of work to be done in fitting normal footplating, etc.

The design of the main frames followed conventional lines. The difference between the design for a 4–6–0 and a 4–6–2 is caused by the widely spaced longitudinal lifting centres. One endeavours to get these as close as possible in order to minimise the bending moment. In a 2–6–4 Tank engine one can drop the lifting slings through the cab roof and pick up the frame just behind the firebox, but in a 4–6–2 the span is bigger, although lifting points are at front of smoke-

box and behind firebox. As mentioned above, the designer uses the boiler strength to reinforce that of the frame. Thus there is a solid fixing on the stretcher, front of the leading driving axle, and a main sliding support at the front of foundation ring and behind the trailing driving axle. The latter was drawn out by L. Barraclough, who had come to Derby D.O. via Horwich and Crewe D.O's, and, when at the N.B. Loco. Co. a few years previously, had detailed the frames for the LNER 'Sandringhams'. He got out a typical Contract Shop design used on Indian State and colonial engines, in which the base of the foundation ring rests on a shoe free to slide longitudinally, but not transversely, and also has two retaining lugs keyed to the frame stretcher.

The main frame plates are sufficiently strong in the vertical plane to permit being lifted with cross-stretchers *in situ*—minus wheels, axles and hornclips; the ties to the boiler give it the structural stiffness of a beam to resist frame deflection when lifting the loco. for transfer down the shop, or for wheeling and unwheeling, etc.

Opinion about the design of the frame structure has oscillated between the 'flexible' and the 'rigid' ideas in the horizontal plane. The maintenance investigators at the formation of the LMSR decided to cut out the pin-jointed cross stays at the hornblock bottoms (as they did the centre bearings) used on the LNWR. By Stanier's time many new classes of loco. had returned to the ideas of cross-stays, but fixed solid by bolts or studs. Likewise the use of horizontal stays running from front to rear (as far as possible) came and went. Much mathematical and statistical work was done by the rather modestly-sized Research Dept. of the early '30s. One cannot determine that it had much effect

permanently. A point that seems to have been overlooked in some of the arguments is the fact that, in years gone by, it was customary to have a $\frac{3}{8}$ in. thick foot plate with outside ('running') angle 5 in. × $2\frac{1}{2}$ in.—to quote LSWR practice. When, in later designs, this was cut down by half, or more, a lot of horizontal stiffness just disappeared. Again, a few years ago, axles had collars against which axleboxes bore and transferred side thrust direct to the main frame concerned, instead of having it passed through frame stretchers from the face of the wheel bearing against the axlebox on the far side, this latter being the case with collar-less axles.

In the case of the present locos, $1\frac{1}{8}$ in. thick frame plates, high tensile steel, were used. These are tied at the front by the buffer beam, reinforced to resist damage from small collisions that often occur in shed yards, but not intended to withstand heavier smashes. Behind this comes the solid block of the inside cylinder casting. Then, between the upper sections, is a small cast steel stretcher forming a saddle for the smokebox and having passages for exhaust steam, from each outside cylinder, from an elbow on the inside cylinder, and one for exhaust steam to the injector. Below, at the base of the frame is the stretcher carrying the bogie centre pivot and, outside the frames, the brackets transferring vertical weight to the bogie 'spittoons'. Slightly behind, and above, is the vertical inside motion plate carrying the rear end of the inside slidebars. From the top of this a line, more or less continuous, of horizontal stretchers runs above the coupled axles. The next vertical stretcher takes the main boiler barrel support: its top face carries a liner whose thickness is determined at assembly. The flanges of the bracket on boiler and on stretcher are bolted up solid. In designing early Stanier locos, the

Above No 46257 *City of Salford* with interim British Railways black livery. The last two 'Duchesses' built, Nos 46256/7 differed slightly in detail to their sisters, notably reversing arrangements, large hopper ashpan, lighter cast steel pony truck and roller bearings on all coupled wheels. It may also be seen that the cab side sheets were noticeably shorter.

Below No 6254 *City of Stoke-on-Trent* in LMS 1946 black livery with maroon and straw lining.
Photos by London Midland Region (B.R.)

D.O. had been impressed by an instruction to copy GW practice in regard to the tops of frame stretchers, and when they saw photographs of GW tank engines in particular, they were puzzled at the way in which the top of the stretcher between outside motion plates disappeared within the bottom of the boiler clothing. They were told that this was done to provide "support if the boiler dropped". How the boiler was to 'drop' they could not guess, but, wishing to be co-operative, the stretchers on the 5X's and 2-6-4 tanks duly had the top beading of their stretchers disappearing within a pocket in the clothing within about 2 in. of the boiler and radiused to match the curve of the boilerplate. The next stretcher, between leading and intermediate driving axles is in line with rear of outside motion girder, and the next between driving and trailing coupled axles carries the rear barrel support at the top and a base-plate for the brake cylinder fixing at the base. Behind the trailing coupled axle the main $1\frac{1}{8}$ in. frames are joined to two hind frame plates. The inner pair bend inwards and are fixed to the hind dragbox and buffer beam. The outer pair bend outwards, but stays tie them to the inner frames and provide seatings for brackets transmitting vertical weight to the pony truck 'spittoons'. The joint in these plates is made by turned rivets, a driving fit in the holes and riveted over cold. At this joint also is the stretcher providing the base for the support at the foundation ring, already described, and, underneath, a base for the pony truck pivot pin buckle and bracket.

The openings in the frame for axlebox guides had a large radius in the top corners and plate edges were fully rounded in order to eliminate any marks in this highly stressed portion from which flaws might start. The guides themselves

were bolted to the main frames. The frames might well have been spaced to come on the centreline of bearings: the figure of 4 ft $1\frac{1}{2}$ in. is more in line with narrow firebox designs where one squeezes the frame between the backs of tyres (about 4 ft $5\frac{1}{2}$ in.) and the firebox outside plates (about 4 ft $0\frac{1}{2}$ in. width). However, I doubt personally whether there is all that in the 'in-line' fashion, associated with the name of Bulleid.

The coupled springs were manufactured from ribbed sectioned alloy steel and were assembled more on a machine shop basis than that of the smith shop outlook. The plates were locked in the buckles by packing pieces and tapered wedge piece seal-welded in position. The span of Stanier springs was longer than previously: a softer ride and lower stresses were hoped for.

J-brackets and screwed spring links were specified although the earlier GW style of equalising beams was not proceeded with. Various types of rocking washers between link and spring end were tried over the years, from those with a sharp V seat to those having a large radiused seat which was supposed to allow the two members to roll on each other. All this was due to persistent breakage of spring links. The shape of thread varied from 'Whitworth' to 'Knuckle' for the same reason. Compression links are disliked in many quarters, but they have many advantages over the tension type, chiefly in the matter of accessibility. In my own apprenticeship days, a fitter and myself had the job of getting an Adams 0-4-4 tank ready for un-wheeling. Adam's engines all had screwed links in tension and J-brackets, and to get the engine ready for lifting we had to remove nuts on links, drop hornblock stays and also the motion. We spent all one afternoon on one pair of spring links: the lock nuts came off easily—

evidently they had not been doing their job—but the main nuts refused to budge in spite of a long tube on a three-foot spanner: and heating up the nuts had no effect. We finally had to split the nuts with cold chisel and flogging hammer. Even if all goes well the lifting requires the springs to be angled to get them in and out of position—a most exasperating job. Drummond engines had 'he and she' screwed compression links, the MR solid compression links, but both required the engine weight to be taken off to adjust them. Urie (really Finlayson, his chief draughtsman) used links in compression but screwed to have nut and washer bearing on the spring end shoe. These could be adjusted under load: the type appeared for a short time on LMS locos. The whole argument depends on how frequently adjustment is made: the answer is probably only at main shoppings. This would favour MR fixed link practice. Of course, in days gone by, case hardening of ends was common: discontinuance of this on spring links (and on motion parts) due to expense, would cause maintenance costs to rise—another case of 'gaining on the swings and losing on the roundabouts'. One further disadvantage of the tension link set-up is the bending and twisting on the J-bracket itself. This loosens the fixing rivets in the end.

Axle-box hornblock or guide clips are another feature causing much worry to designers. Whether to clip the frame or the guide foot or both seems to be the question and how to prevent the clips coming loose. In the present case ordinary horizontal clips with lips were used.

The manufacture of the frames followed normal practice; levelling, profiling and drilling in batches with the use of jigs. Being small orders, Crewe shops did not have a fixed frame stand or jig as

Above LMS No 6202, the Turbomotive locomotive was re-built in 1952 as a conventional Pacific and named *Princess Anne*. In this form, the locomotive perished in the 1952 tragedy at Harrow, after only a few months in service. Pictured here at Shrewsbury.
Photo by W. Potter.

Below No 46220 *Coronation* awaiting departure from Glasgow Central with the 10.05 to Birmingham, watches the departure of the up 'The Royal Scot'. 25/7/59.
Photo by Douglas Doherty.

they had for the building of Horwich 2–6–0's (Crabs), which was one of Beames's impressive ideas, but built the frames and stretchers up on adjustable stands. The frames are lined up, with horn-clips in position, stretchers added, etc. The axlebox guide faces are checked up for transverse alignment and squareness with cylinder centres. The cylinder front faces are checked by fixed length gauge and trammels, with a straight edge giving true axlebox centre-line positions. Jig drilling simplifies the correct positioning of the larger details and minimises constructional errors.

It is important that motion plate and brackets carrying the motion girder ends are true and square. At the same time the motion plate and valve spindle guide castings must line up with the incline of the cylinders. Across the two frame plates the faces for reversing shaft brackets have also to be checked. Two other sets of fixed points require careful checking: the brackets transmitting vertical weight at the bogie and at the pony truck.

In order to save time in scribing the centre-line of axles in the horn gaps at repair, datum buttons on the horizontal centre-line and at a standard distance to right and left of hornblock or guide are fitted on the main frames. The line scribed on them is centre-popped and used as a reference point at repairs. Thus, either the liner on the axlebox guide or the face of the axlebox itself can be machined or ground to bring the axle box back central again.

The 4-wheeled bogie was specified to be the same as for 'Princess Royal'. It was, of course, pure GWR style but only on 4–6–2's did the LMS use it. It is strange to note in passing that, later on, Swindon design became 'LMS ised' on the Hawksworth 'Counties' to the extent of having the LMS 2–8–0 boiler, plate frame

bogie, 'slap-on' outside cylinders and main frame running through to front buffer beam, and that this took place before 'Nationalisation' started injecting 'foreign' personnel. The bogie for the 'Coronation' and 'Duchesses' had top and bottom bar frames with axlebox guides bolted to their inside faces acting as spacers. Across, and fixed to, the two top bars was the cross stretcher on which the centre slide moved, as operated by the projecting centre pin attached to the engine main frame stretcher, its transverse movement being resisted by the slide and the bogie cross stretcher, having, as already stated, to accommodate a movement of $2\frac{3}{4}$ in. each way. Weight transfer from the loco. main frames is by the brackets already mentioned into 'spittoons' sliding on the top face of the bogie cross stretcher. Thence the weight is passed to an inverted laminated spring whose buckle spigots into the underside of the bogie cross stretcher and thence, by links, to pins in the equalising beam whose ends rest on the axlebox tops. It is a very neat, compact design with only one drawback, i.e. that, due to the laminated spring buckle having a spherical end, the bogie frame did at times run crabwise, 'up' against the axlebox bottom at the front and 'down' against the top at the back. The substitution of a square face instead of the spherical end cured this. It is incredible to think that Swindon used to have a vacuum brake cylinder and blocks on both sides of the wheels on this bogie too. A masterpiece of designing! The LMS practice was also to fit Ferobestos liners under the 'spittoons' to stop bogie hunting.

The two-wheeled Bissel truck in essentials followed examples given in the American Locomotive Dictionary, a volume found in many D.O's. Its design had originally been prepared for the 4–6–2

Compound, proposed during the Fowler regime of the LMS and seemed heavy and cumbersome. The LMS appears to have favoured Bissel trucks rather than radial axles; the MR had boxes of drawings of the Schenectady and Baldwin 2–6–0's still in the D.O. stores in the '20s. It is possible that the design of the leading trucks of the S & D 2–8–0, MR 2–6–4, and even Horwich Crab came from them. In the present design a feature was made of transmitting vertical loads to 'spittoons', with Ferobestos liners directly above axle box centres. Likewise control springs for side movement were on line of axle. Laminated bearing springs had rocking washers, rubber pads and screwed links.

The amount and arrangement of side control spring loading on bogies and pony trucks has received much attention, theoretical and practical. A lot of test runs took place on the now lost Hassop/Bakewell curves, which were specially superelevated for 75 m.p.h., by a 2–6–4 LMS tank fitted up with so called flange force recorders. One difficulty in assessing results is to separate flange force from tread friction. The point of the exercise and of theoretical investigation was to find a correct control spring value which would ensure that guiding by bogies, etc., was really carried out and side forces on coupled wheels reduced. Actually during the 1914/18 war we ran one of Drummond's larger 4–4–0's (the 463's) with one side control spring only, as we could not get the bits and pieces to repair the other for a week: the usual loading in those days was 1 ton initial, 2 tons final. Latterly, they have been as high as 5 and 6 tons respectively. On a 4–6–2 it appears contrary to control the Bissel which is operating against the loading at the bogie. Experience seems to indicate that all axles should be controlled from 'wandering' on the straight. GW practice, on their early 4-6-0's, was to fit 'Cartazzi' inclined slides on the trailing coupled axleboxes to allow controlled side movement. As already stated, bogie side movement was $2\frac{3}{4}$ in. each way and loading is usually given as 4 tons initial, 5 tons final loading: and for the pony truck $4\frac{1}{4}$ in. each way with 1·44 tons initial and 2·96 tons final.

All wheels had the stiff triangular section of rim, shrunk-on tyres, and Gibson retaining rings. They were pressed on to axles using the usual methods; coupled wheels were keyed on in addition. The axles themselves were hollow-bored to save weight. The wheel seat position is greater in diameter than the journal in order to keep any flaws from developing therein unseen. The crank axle was of the built-up type. Crank pins are also pressed-in; care is taken that the angle of the driving pin is correct for the return crank attachment.

The practice of balancing wheels is well known. In the present case weights are attached to each crank pin to simulate those of coupling rods, etc. The decision concerning reciprocating weights—pistons, etc., and part of connecting rods— was to balance 50%. Finally the lead is run into pockets formed by plates riveted across the spokes. The drawing office works out what is required from information from wheel shop of the weights— in the form of steel plates fixed by nuts and bolts—that they found necessary to attach to the wheels to secure freedom from vibration of the wheel-and-axle assembly on the balancing machine.

The axleboxes for coupled wheels were steel castings with pressed-in brasses, white-metal lined. A feature is that lubrication came from grooves at practically the horizontal centre-line and oil pads below. The oil feed was at the box top and passed through passages at the back of the brass to the grooves. The keeps containing the oil pads, where clearance allowed, were removeable by sliding out of axlebox horizontally. The spring hangers were placed below out of the way. The bearing centre-line was also that of the guide face; the axlebox flanges here were chamfered to allow the engine to roll. Faces to the wheel centres were large and white-metalled, as were those bearing against the guides.

The axleboxes for carrying wheels were conventional alloy castings with removeable under-keeps and oil pads; no mechanical or top lubrication was provided.

Dust shields were fitted on the open sides of all axleboxes. Endeavours were made to seal the gap on the opposite side, but nothing materialised.

The vertical loading on the carrying axles was between 150 and 200 lbs per sq. in. and on the drivers about 250 lb. per sq. in. This will increase with wear. For the same reason the stress is kept low and failure of axles on rare occasions is usually due to flaws being set up.

The early scheme had a general

No 46255 *City of Hereford* leaving Rugby with an express from Euston to Perth and Blackpool on 30/8/58. *Photo by Douglas Doherty.*

No 46231 *Duchess of Atholl* leaving
Euston in 1953 heading 'The Royal Scot'.
Photo by London Midland Region (B.R.).

idea as to the layout of the valve motion. In most designs there is a lack of space, horizontally and transversely. One usually sets up on the drawing board one or two cross-sections showing, guide, mainframe, springs, wheels, crank pins and coupling rods. On a Walschaert gear the expansion link and its bearings are often a tight squeeze within the loading gauge. One also has to watch that the off-sets of rods in plan are kept to a minimum. It is a good rule to keep the swing of the expansion link down to 45°: although this may mean a longer link, it keeps the slip of the die block down. A curious feature of Walschaert's gear seems to be that more equal readings of events at front and back strokes of piston is obtained with the radius rod working at the top of the link: for which reason the SE and CR 2–6–0 and 2–6–4's of Maunsell era had their 'fore-gear' position thus, whereas normally one prefers to have a straight through drive with the radius rod in the lower half of the link. Rocking levers are more common working in the vertical plane, e.g. with piston valves placed above cylinders with Stephenson valve gear, and are usually with arms at 180°. Those working in a horizontal plane are also usually at 180° but the GW had theirs 'off set'. When the 'Coronation' gear was set up on the valve motion model various off-sets were tried but one could not see much advantage in the valve readings in so doing and therefore the 180° position was adopted. The 'kick' from the die block to the radius rod in the 'Royal Scots' had caused it to strike the expansion link on occasion—possibly due to driver's running the gear down to 'full gear' when coasting—but also due to spring in the reversing shaft. The valve motion on the 'Coronations' was a different layout from that on the 'Princesses' and nearer

that of the outside 'Scot' motion: therefore a better design than the 'Scot' was required now.

A young man, D. M. Wilcox, was given the job of designing the reversing gear—like other 'bright young men' from Horwich, he soon left railway employment for something more promising. He proposed a much lighter pattern girder with plummer blocks carrying the expansion link. At the back end, a reversing shaft of large diameter, but hollow bored, was arranged, with bell-crank at left-hand end, one arm carrying the sliding block in radius rod extension, the other connected to reversing screw. At right-hand end one arm only for the sliding block connection. The shaft was in two portions, for ease in assembly, with flanged and spigotted couplings.

On the last engines the reversing screw and its bracket were placed on a support bracket front of the wide firebox, where all reacting forces would be absorbed, leaving only a rotating tube connecting to the wheel in the cab to be required. This was far superior to the arrangement on the 'Princesses' where an intermediate shaft was necessary to allow the reversing rod to pass the wide firebox and all vibrations finally being passed to a conventional screw and bracket mounted on a not-too-stiff cab-toolbox.

The slidebars, being supported near their centres, departed from the previous 'crocodile' style and were fluted, rectangular. The crossheads had no separate slippers but were castings white-metalled on wearing surfaces. The piston rod coned end was solid-bottomed into the crosshead, i.e. with no draw, and cottered with the small end of cotter outside. Box-type expansion link and the valve gear generally followed LMS practice; also the return crank fixed on the crank pin end by 4-studs. True, this had a spigot, but it may seem remarkable that, although it had to

be removed whenever the connecting and/or coupling rods were to be removed apparently no case of any working loose on any of the hundreds of LMS locos using this feature took place. The two departures from previous designs were in the fact that the coupling rods were fluted instead of hitherto rectangular section and that the valve spindle slides were carried on a frame bracket instead of being supported from below on the back steam chest cover. This arrangement makes for easy adjustment when wear has taken place. As has already been mentioned, a horizontal 1 to 1 lever with arms at 180° transmitted the valve motion from the outside gear to the inside valve spindle by means of a long rod inside and two 5 in. links on the outside valve spindle extension.

As originally fitted up all pin joints had needle roller bearings. For some years a ball bearing (in the usual cage) had been used on return crank pins, but needle bearings had no cage to hold them together should the inner or outer races be removed intentionally or accidentally. Nevertheless, Doncaster had written good reports of their experience with Ransome and Marles type and it was decided to fit Hoffman's type on the 'Coronations'. In some positions, i.e. the die block in the expansion link, space was so small that no inner race could be provided. Here, the needles bore straight on to the pin: If the pin were carelessly removed the needles scattered far and wide. A further complication arose when wear had taken place and replacements were required: it can be imagined how difficult this would be to control. Very soon after the outbreak of World War II any bearings of this sort were unobtainable for civilian jobs and the former style of bronze bushes with oiling rings on the motion links became standard once more.

The cylinders are iron castings;

they have straight ports, beloved of the theorists but a worry for the foundry. The straight walls, as compared with those slightly curved, are apt to become highly stressed between the body of the cylinder and that of the steam chest as they cool off after casting and flaws are not unknown. The vertical centre-lines, in the designing, are kept as close as possible—bearing in mind removal of cylinder cover and piston head—so keeping down clearance volume. The bridge pieces across the ports at the liner bore were shaped to help direct the flow of steam and the port shape itself designed so that its area grew in relation to the feeding area of the liner ports. The liner bores were slightly different in diameter—the far one being slightly smaller than the near one.

The piston valves were similar and so one did not have to drive the valve spindle and valves through two bores one after the other. The passages to the saddle were easily arranged to decrease evenly in cross-section in the outside cylinder but this was not so easy on the inside cylinder due to lack of space. The piston valve head was also 'streamlined' in the body with a shaped false cover on the outer sides. It had the usual six narrow rings.

The valve motion itself was designed for valves having $1\frac{3}{4}$ in. lap, and a maximum opening to steam port also $1\frac{3}{4}$ in., and a lead of $\frac{1}{4}$ in. This requires a travel in full gear of 7 in. By the time the gear is 'notched up' to about 50% the travel will have come down by a third, the opening to steam by

two-thirds, and the exhaust port will just be fully used, i.e. its $1\frac{3}{4}$ in. width fully open. It is interesting to see how the lead opening becomes of increasing value as the gear is notched up—for which reason the writer advocated $\frac{5}{16}$ in. lead; and also that by widening the valve head and port width in sympathy an even better opening to exhaust is obtainable at mid and long cut-off's. Earlier Stanier locos, had run with $\frac{1}{4}$ in. clearance between piston head and cylinder cover. This had proved too much a policy of perfection for the LMS and the 'Coronations' had the more usual $\frac{3}{8}$ in. clearance. The piston head itself, however, still had the tapered screwed GW type fixing. The percentage cut-offs were indicated by a pointer to figures marked on a rotating

With the journey almost completed, No 46253 *City of St. Albans* coasts down Camden bank into Euston with the up 'The Royal Scot'. 15/8/60.
Photo by Douglas Doherty.

Running light, tender first, from Manchester back to Crewe is No 46233 *Duchess of Sutherland*. She had earlier worked down with a Euston–Manchester express. 17/4/59, at Stockport.
Photo by Douglas Doherty.

drum, part of the drivers 'reversing' screw assembly in the cab.

Whether streamlining was fitted or not the cab had a 'peaked' front plate. Side windows of ample size were a feature of Stanier locos and the front ones were inclined, so cutting out reflections. All opened to facilitate cleaning. A sliding ventilator was fitted in the roof and no more than the necessary gauges were fitted. A normal fall-plate and cab doors were also fitted.

The programme for mechanising routine work at running sheds has already been mentioned and one consequence was the necessity to design drop grates and hopper ashpans. These appeared on the 'Coronations' and suffered much change in design in order to try and provide equipment that would stand up to rough usage and much abuse. Perhaps the design could have been done better by a steel works or agricultural machinery office than by a loco office, except for the fact that weight and accessibility were at a premium—old friends of the L.D.O's. A drop grate, with removable lever in cab, was provided and ultimately two ashpan hopper doors, arranged at an angle to help ash and fire clearance, were fitted. Two doors for air admission in the usual way were fitted, one at front and one at back.

Other more congenial 'self-service' features included atomised mechanical lubrication to valves and cylinders; plain mechanical lubrication to axleboxes and grease lubrication to motion parts. Steam sanding to the coupled wheels and steam cylinders operating cylinder cocks, also fitted, had appeared on other Stanier designs in place of hand operating gear.

The tender ran on roller bearing axleboxes. It was large for a 6-wheeled chassis and intended to carry 10 tons of coal. A coal pusher was mounted on the top rear tank. This was another piece of rough machinery that never seemed to reach successful development, probably due to a wish to keep it simple whereas the problem to be solved demanded complicated movements.

The usual steam carriage warming services were provided: the reducing valve on the boiler back was a very neat design based on principles enunciated some years previously by D. W. Sanford. Another LMS practice was the fitting of steam brake on engine and tender. The argument in its favour —as against vacuum or air pressure —being that, as it is important to be able to stop the loco if it can be started, time should not be wasted in creating vacuum or air pressure, but steam, being available, should be used at once. The braking of guiding wheels had been considered 'dangerous' in the '20s, but double blocks were now fitted on one side of the coupled wheels.

For some reason or other, the design of this loco went through the offices with enthusiasm and little argument. Possibly this was due to the feeling that, for once, it was made up of the D.O.'s own ideas and, with Coleman on the spot and Stanier in India, they 'pleased themselves' to a greater extent. The building was all done at Crewe Works and a very fine job they turned out. At the conclusion, Coleman took his men to see No 6220 finished in the Paint Shop at Crewe. Many years later on, he paid visits to the level crossing north of Tamworth station to see her on the Up 'Scot' train.

After World War II ended the last two locos of the class were turned out. These differed slightly in detail from the earlier non-streamlined locos; reversing arrangement, large hopper ashpan, lighter cast steel pony truck and roller bearings on all coupled wheels. Visually the cab side sheets were shorter also. Rumour had it that they were to run 'in competition' with 10,000 and 10,001 Diesel electrics from an accountant's point of view. It would appear that the march of events overtook this intention for nothing was published apart from some first costs.

No. 6202 Turbomotive at Shrewsbury
Photo by W. Potter

Principal Dimensions
Cylinders: (4) 16½ in. diameter 28 in. stroke
Coupled Wheels: 6 ft 9 in. diameter
Leading Bogie Wheels: 3 ft 0 in. diameter
Trailing Bissel Wheels: 3 ft 9 in. diameter
Wheelbase—Coupled: 14 ft 6 in. Total Engine: 37 ft 0 in.
Boiler Pressure: 250 lb per sq. in.
Boiler Barrel Diameter (Max.): 6 ft 5½ in.
Firebox, Outside: 8 ft 6 in. long, 7 ft 6⅝ in. tapering to 7 ft 0¼ in. wide
Tubes Superheater Elements: 40 (triple) 1 in. diameter outside
Large Tubes: 40 × 5⅛ in. diameter outside ⎫
Small Tubes: 129 × 2⅜ in. diameter outside ⎬ 19 ft 3 in. between tube plates
Heating Surface—
Tubes: 2,577 sq. ft Firebox: 230 sq. ft Superheater: 830 sq. ft
Grate Area: 50 sq. ft
Tractive Effort at 85% B.P.: 40,000 lb

LMS LOCOMOTIVES 6220–57

Weights (Official)

	Light:	Loaded:
Engine	95–10–0	105– 5–0
Tender	29–10–0	56– 7–0
Total	124– 0–0	161–12–0

Adhesion Factor: 3·73

No.	Name	Date built	Original condition and livery		Date of Withdrawal
6220	*Coronation*	1937	Streamlined	Blue and silver	4/63
6221	*Queen Elizabeth*	1937	,,	,,	5/63
6222	*Queen Mary*	1937	,,	,,	10/63
6223	*Princess Alice*	1937	,,	,,	10/63
6224	*Princess Alexandra*	1937	,,	,,	10/63
6225	*Duchess of Gloucester*	1938	Streamlined	Maroon and yellow	9/64
6226	*Duchess of Norfolk*	1938	,,	,,	9/64
6227	*Duchess of Devonshire*	1938	,,	,,	12/62
6228	*Duchess of Rutland*	1938	,,	,,	9/64
6229	*Duchess of Hamilton*	1938	,,	,,	2/64
6230	*Duchess of Buccleuch*	1938	Non-streamlined	Maroon and yellow	11/65
6231	*Duchess of Atholl*	1938	,,	,,	12/62
6232	*Duchess of Montrose*	1938	,,	,,	12/62
6233	*Duchess of Sutherland*	1938	,,	,,	2/64
6234	*Duchess of Abercorn*	1938	,,	,,	1/63
6235	*City of Birmingham*	1939	Streamlined	Maroon and yellow	9/64
6236	*City of Bradford*	1939	,,	,,	3/64
6237	*City of Bristol*	1939	,,	,,	9/64
6238	*City of Carlisle*	1939	,,	,,	9/64
6239	*City of Chester*	1939	,,	,,	9/64
6240	*City of Coventry*	1940	,,	,,	9/64
6241	*City of Edinburgh*	1940	,,	,,	9/64
6242	*City of Glasgow*	1940	,,	,,	10/63
6243	*City of Lancaster*	1940	,,	,,	9/64
6244	*King George VI*	1940	,,	,,	9/64
6245	*City of London*	1943	Streamlined	Wartime black	9/64
6246	*City of Manchester*	1943	,,	,,	1/63
6247	*City of Liverpool*	1943	,,	,,	5/63
6248	*City of Leeds*	1943	,,	,,	9/64
6249	*City of Sheffield*	1944	Non-streamlined	Wartime black	11/63
6250	*City of Lichfield*	1944	,,	,,	9/64
6251	*City of Nottingham*	1944	,,	,,	9/64
6252	*City of Leicester*	1944	,,	,,	6/63
6253	*City of St. Albans*	1946	Non-streamlined	Postwar LMS black	1/63
6254	*City of Stoke-on-Trent*	1946	,,	,,	9/64
6255	*City of Hereford*	1946	,,	,,	9/64
6256	*Sir William A. Stanier, F.R.S.*	1947	,,	,,	10/64
6257	*City of Salford*	1948	Non-streamlined tender lettered 'British Railways'.	Postwar LMS black,	9/64

All the locomotives were built at Crewe   Preserved are Nos. 6229, 6233, and 6235

Above In red and yellow livery, No 6227 *Duchess of Devonshire* at Polmadie in 1938.
Photo by T. G. Hepburn.

Below Coming off Polmadie M.P.D. is No 46223 *Princess Alice.* Note the very carefully trimmed coal on the tender. 24/7/59.
Photo by Douglas Doherty.

The LMS Duchesses—
a performance evaluation

by JOHN POWELL, C.Eng., B.Sc (Eng)., M.I.Mech.E.

It seldom does any harm, and usually clears the air, if a commentator makes a declaration of interest at the outset. Let me begin, therefore, by saying that in my view the ex-LMS 'Duchess' was the finest express passenger locomotive to run in Britain. This has been my considered view, often expressed to innumerable colleagues, for many years.

Now let me qualify that statement. There was one other class of locomotive in this country which ran it a close second: I refer, of course, to the rebuilt 'Merchant Navy'. Then it must be conceded that the A4's did very fine work which was every bit the equal of what the 'Duchesses' were normally called upon to do. The environment of these other locomotives—

the current schedules and loadings, the nature of the routes, the *esprit-de-corps* of the enginemen and operating staff, even line tradition—sometimes enabled them to put up performances which surpassed good 'Duchess' work. Nevertheless, I unhesitatingly maintain that these, the biggest of the LMS passenger designs, were the most capable of all express passenger locomotives in Britain.

The environmental factors warrant further examination. On the LM Region lines, train loadings and corresponding timings were generally laid down in four scales (though some lines, by their nature, could not be covered by the faster timings). These were, in ascending speed order, 'Full Load', 'Limited Load', 'Special

Limit' and 'XL Limit'. Ignoring the 'Full Load' timings, which were usually confined to special and dated summer trains, class 8P engines such as the 'Duchesses' were allowed the following tare loads between Euston and Crewe, for instance, in relation to the start-to-stop timings shown:

	Load, tons	Start-to-stop timing, minutes
Limited load	655	176
Special limit	600	165
XL limit	510	155

Now except during wartime (when the more restrictive timings were not used anyway) it was unusual for loadings to exceed 16 coaches on any service, which

One of the first batch of non-streamlined 'Duchesses', No 6230 *Duchess of Buccleuch* running into Crewe with an up express in 1938.
Photo by T. G. Hepburn.

TABLE 1. Up 'Ulster Express': 6.55 a.m. Heysham–Euston (1954) (XL Limit Timings)

Locomotive: Cl.8P 4–6–2 No 46242 *City of Glasgow*
Load: 10 coaches, 323 tons tare, 345 tons gross
Driver: H. J. Jones: Fireman: N. Hayward (Crewe N)

Dist. miles		Sched. mins.	Actual m s	Speeds m.p.h.	Boiler press.	Reg.	Cut off
0·0	CREWE	0	0 00	—	225	FV	25
	Basford Hall Junc.		4 33	—	230	,,	..
4·8	Betley Road		9 05	47	225	,,	..
8·0	Madeley		13 10	48	210	,,	..
10·5	Whitmore	15	15 44	55	230	,,	18
14·7	Standon Bridge		19 43	68	230	,,	..
			p.w.s.			shut	—
19·2	Norton Bridge	23	24 30	72/22	225	FV	30
		4		68½	230	shut	—
24·5	STAFFORD	33	30 43	—	—	—	—
			p.w.s.	17	215	FV	20
28·6	Milford	37	38 34	—	—	,,	..
30·9	Colwich		41 18	62	225	,,	..
			p.w.s.			shut	
33·8	RUGELEY	42	45 08	15	230	FV	40
37·1	Armitage		50 11	60½	210	,,	20
			p.w.s.			shut	—
41·8	LICHFIELD	49	56 08	63/21	210	FV	40
44·6	Hademore		59 49	63	200	,,	20
48·1	TAMWORTH	55	63 13	60	225	,,	..
51·6	Polesworth		66 31	66	225	,,	..
55·8	Atherstone		70 30	62	210	,,	..
61·0	NUNEATON	67	75 14	69	190	shut	—
			p.w.s.	20	215	FV	40/25
66·7	Shilton		83 48	58	215	,,	20
70·0	Brinklow		86 47	68	210	,,	..
	Newbold		89 28	65	215	shut	—
			p.w.s.	22			
75·5	RUGBY	82	93 43	—	215	FV	32
77·8	Hillmorton		96 44	48	225	,,	20
82·8	Welton		102 17	56/65	215	,,	..
88·4	Weedon	94	106 59	71/65	220	,,	..
95·3	Blisworth	100	113 00	74	200	,,	..
98·2	Roade	103	115 37	67½	225	shut	—
			p.w.s.	25	220	FV	25
103·3	Castlethorpe		121 38	57	—	,,	20
105·7	Wolverton		124 08	66	—	,,	..
111·4	BLETCHLEY	114	129 21	67/71	205	,,	..
117·9	Leighton Buzzard		134 49	74	220	,,	15
122·0	Cheddington		138 17	69	220	,,	..
126·4	TRING	128	142 19	63	225	,,	..
130·1	Berkhamsted	4	145 41	71	225	Breath	15
133·6	Hemel Hempstead	4	148 39	69	225	,,	..
137·2	Kings Langley		151 46	69	—	,,	..
140·7	WATFORD JUNC.	144	154 49	67	—	shut	—
			sig. stop*				
142·2	Bushey		158 07	—	225	FV	50/25
144·8	Hatch End	4	161 59	62	—	,,	25
146·7	Harrow		—	70	—	,,	..
	Sudbury Junc.		166 43	72/64	—	shut	—
152·7	WILLESDEN JUNC.	159	169 11	63	—	FV	25
157·1	Camden No. 1	2	174 32	30	—	shut	—
159·1	EUSTON	169	177 40	—			

* Signal cleared but unable to release brakes in time.   Water consumption: 5.900 gallons = 37·2 gallons per mile.

No 46242 *City of Glasgow* on Kingmoor M.P.D. on 16/6/63. This locomotive was involved in the Harrow collision of 1952, and is here shown re-built with full curved footplating at the front. *Photo by W. Potter.*

with BR standard stock could amount to about 535 tons tare; most of the faster trains were kept down to about 13 coaches, or something like 435 tons. Clearly, except on a few hard workings, such as the 7.55 a.m. Euston–Liverpool and Manchester train in the late '50s (of which more later) there was a very ample margin of power available on demand with the 'Duchesses'.

In looking at their performance, too, one must see it against a background of often indifferent operating, the progressive interference with free running by the West Coast main line electrification work south of Crewe, and a widespread lowering of morale as the introduction of diesels made steam locomotive enginemanship less attractive and firing skills began to evaporate for lack of practice. The 'get-up-and-go' attitude had not been strong and widespread

on the Western Division of the LM Region since before the war—with honourable exceptions—and undoubtedly there was a lot of easy-going train running as a result, even when there was every need for more effort. I recall a Camden driver, as we backed down from the shed to work the 2.40 p.m. Liverpool about 1952, watching the Bushbury crew on the 2.25 p.m. Wolverhampton come pounding up Camden bank with a 'Jubilee' on ten and saying "Just look at those silly b....s, knocking hell out of it like that".

As a prime example of what I mean, Table 1 records a trip I made in 1954 on the footplate of the Up 'Ulster Express' from Crewe to Euston. The engine had worked through from Morecambe, but Crewe North men took over at Crewe and we were away to time. The load was no more than 345 tons gross, well within the 'XL

Limit' loadings for the train, and the basic timing of 155 minutes was increased by a total of 14 minutes recovery time. Despite a known 7 permanent way slacks en route, there was no reason why this train should not have been worked within overall time; the engine was in fine shape apart from the safety valves blowing off light, coal was decent, and the fireman experienced.

But what happened? We wandered along to Rugby on the first valve only of the regulator—I estimate the equivalent D.B.H.P. up to Madeley at only 1,185—only touching the 70 m.p.h. mark once briefly, and by that point were $11\frac{3}{4}$ minutes late. By Roade, unchecked, the lateness had further increased and even after the seventh slack and passing Bletchley $15\frac{1}{4}$ minutes down the driver had still not woken up to the fact that the first valve was not good enough.

So we made a modest climb to Tring—any 'Jubilee' could have done as well—before dawdling down to Willesden. The driver was clearly one who would not *run*—and he was presumably allowed to get away with it.

However, I am jumping the gun. First, a look at where it all happens—the footplate.

Cab Layout

The 'Duchess' footplate was not really very much more imposing than that of, say, a Class 5, and the layout was very similar, though the level was a little higher. The great width of the firebox was, of course, immediately noticeable, and this very feature caused a variation from the normal Stanier screw reverse, in that it was necessary to gear the screw to get the reach rod out along the side of the firebox. A reduction ratio was considered desirable, and as a result a fair amount of winding was involved to get from full forward to full back gear. As on almost all LMS designs (the 'Crabs' and 'Patriots' were the only exceptions that occur to me) a crossbar with two handles, one of which hinged to operate the catch, was used instead of a reversing wheel.

Again, as a result of the wide firebox the cab front windows were fairly narrow, and this, plus the bulge at the firebox throatplate, and the smoke deflectors, made for a very restricted forward view. The use of the glass draught deflector screens on the outside of the cab was almost obligatory.

Because of the width and restricted view, the regulator handle, of normal Stanier quadrant pattern with spring catch to engage the 'drifting' and 'full-open' positions, was rather longer than usual. It was unlikely to stay put in any position between 'drifting' and full-open', because of its weight and the running vibration, and so a wooden wedge carried by the driver, or a carefully selected piece of coal, was habitually inserted between the handle and the quadrant stop.

The normal Stanier steam sanding valve and ejector steam valves were convenient to the driver's right hand. Midland combined vacuum/steam brake valve was above and to the right of the reversing handle, and the cylinder drain cock handle sat against the cab side forward of the tip-up seat.

For the fireman, injector and carriage warming steam valves were mounted on the manifold, while the injector water controls were on the cab sides by the seats. The blower valve occupied the time-honoured Midland position in the centre of the scene above the firehole door—hardly the ideal place in the event of a 'blowback'. Not all these engines had rocking grates, but on those so fitted the three operating stubs were set down below the floor under hinged covers. Damper controls of the pull-up 'walking stick' type were at the right-hand corner of the firebox, on the floor.

The firedoors themselves caused a little difficulty in their time. They were of the sliding type, but were quite thick to allow sufficient secondary air through their hollow structure. Given the least tightness or lack of lubrication in the guides, the offset pull of the operating linkage could cause them to jam, and only the blade of the shovel, or stern treatment with the coal hammer, would liberate them. And I am not talking of the occasions when a chairscrew, inserted to tilt the smoke plate upwards in the firehole, worked back and jammed the doors from the inside!

One item was, of course, unique to these engines; the coal pusher. The steam-operated ram mounted on the bunker slope sheet in the tender was controlled by a miniature regulator handle on the tender front, close to the fireiron tunnel, and worked by up-and-down rotation through 90°, with suitable pauses between movements while the coal heaved its way forward. It was not the most reliable animal, because it had to work under most appalling conditions, but it was a real labour-saver when it *was* working.

Gauges comprised vacuum brake, speedometer (later), boiler pressure and carriage warming pressure. No steam chest pressure gauge, be it noted: you did it by feel and sound!

Preparation and Disposal

The only item of preparation calling for comment was the inside motion. The crossheads and slidebars were awkwardly placed over the bogie centre casting, which quickly became the filthiest part of the locomotive. However, lubrication was a little easier than on the 3-cylinder 4–6–0's, because there were no inside combination levers, and only the slidebar oil-boxes, bottom slidebars and little end oilwells were involved.

Judicious setting of the engine with the inside big ends on the back quarters made the job fairly easy. Careful attention to the inside big ends was essential, and ideally this involved another setting to the bottom quarters.

In disposal, the main area that needed watching was the ashpan, particularly where a rocking grate was fitted. The 'four-ply' construction of the main frames over the truck necessitated rather shallow ashpan slopes, which were not self-cleaning. Buildup of ash and clinker was particularly prone to occur at the front corners, which were difficult to rake through the damper, and this could soon cause burning of the grate by interference with the air supply. The last two engines, with rear bar frame extensions over the truck, allowed the ashpans to be redesigned with generous side raking doors.

Above No 6233 *Duchess of Sutherland* as restored for preservation at Butlins Camp at Ayr. This locomotive is now at Bressingham. Picture taken on 30/8/64.
Photo by W. Potter.

Below Crewe station on 4/8/58. No 46221 *Queen Elizabeth* awaits the arrival of the down 'The Royal Scot' in order to take it forward. 'Princess Royal' class No 46210 *Lady Patricia* passes by on its way to the other end of the station to await the London bound train it will take over.
Photo by Douglas Doherty.

Driving a 'Duchess'

In your hands you had a big, imposing, powerful but sensitive machine; you had to show her who was in charge, or she would very soon take charge of you!

The first thing to remember was that she was very touchy on her feet. The adhesion factor was only 3·73, and even on straight track you could not play the fool with the regulator. On curves and point-work, she could be even less sure-footed, because of weight transfer from the coupled wheels as a result of the action of the bogie and trailing truck.

In addition, the volume of steam in the main steam pipes, 40-element supheater, header and 4 valve chests was very large, so that even after the regulator was closed there was enough uncontrollable steam to feed the 4 cylinders for $1\frac{1}{2}$ revolutions at full pressure in full gear. So, by the time you had realised she was starting to slip, reacted to the idea, closed the regulator and waiting for the steam already past it to be exhausted, she could be AWAY in a spectacular slip. That assumes you could close the regulator; if the water level was high and she started to entrain water with the steam, this could be difficult or impossible until you had wound her into mid-gear and minimised the steam flow, all of which took time.

So the prudent driver, anxious to make a clean start, would put the reverser to about 40% cutoff, open the regulator and close it again immediately, and see if she moved away; then repeat the trick, leaving the regulator open a shade longer this time; if she still did not move, he would drop her down to about 55% and repeat the process. This time it would be most unusual for her not to move, and suggestive that the large ejector might be needed to get a full brake release at the rear of the train. In practice the whole process

as described rarely took longer than 7–8 seconds, and almost certainly saved time in the long run.

Apart from this, a 'Duchess' was a machine you could really become a part of. The riding was superb, free from rolling, vibration or axle knock, easy at high speeds and devoid of any tendency to vicious kicking on curves. Full regulator or first valve, she would do her work competently and economically. Most of her work could be done at 15–18% cutoff, and it was unusual to go above 40% even on Shap or Beattock. For really fast running on a reasonable road, full regulator and 25% was a sure indication that the crew meant business and would not be put off!

Firing

The grate area of 50 sq. ft meant, in the fireman's eyes, a slightly trapezoidal area about 7 ft 9 in. long and 6 ft 9 in. wide at the throat-plate, tapering to about 6 ft 3 in. wide at the doorplate. The rear 3 ft or so were level, and the forward part sloped down at about 1 in $3\frac{3}{4}$. If the firing were done in an arc round the rear half of the perimeter, i.e. mainly on the flat portion, thick in the back corners to match the draught with back damper open and thinning off towards the front and centre, the rest of the grate would well-nigh look after itself with coal shaking forward.

Of course, it is easy to *say* "keep the back corners filled". But you are doing it under the edges of the smoke plate—hence those chair screws!—and pushing it uphill nearly the length of the shovel handle across and close up to the firehole, and that means you have to watch your hands. Many firemen on these engines wore a thick leather glove, or an asbestos welder's glove on the right hand (if they fired left-handed to suit the

footplate) to avoid burning. And they picked their lumps of coal with careful breaking to size, to get largish sizes for the back corners—anything up to a foot long, something you could get the shovel behind and prod into place if necessary—firing the smaller stuff down the sides or just inside the door. Slack inside the door could be dug up with the shovel blade if it tended to cake or become solid.

All this time, of course, the fireman was busy between firings with breaking coal, operating the coal pusher, watching the working of the injector, and brushing and hosing down the footplate, quite apart from spotting the odd signal for the driver. Not exactly a rest cure!

Performance: The Prewar Period

The first Duchess appeared in 1937, and the initial batch of five streamlined engines went on to the 'Coronation Scot' service primarily, with its light-weight $6\frac{1}{2}$ hour working between Euston and Glasgow Central. The remaining engines, as they progressively appeared from Crewe Works, were drafted to general heavy haulage on the Western Division. Nevertheless it is interesting to note that the pages of Cecil J. Allen's articles in the *Railway Magazine* during 1938 and 1939 contain no record (other than the *Duchess of Abercorn* trials in 1939) of their work on trains other than the 'Coronation Scot'. Such is the measure of the command which the 'Princesses' held at that time over the heavy Anglo-Scottish services.

In readiness for the inauguration of the 'Coronation Scot' in July 1937, the LMS Railway laid on a demonstration run from Euston to Crewe and back with its new train on 29 June, for an invited audience of pressmen and others. At this time the British speed record with steam stood at $112\frac{1}{2}$ m.p.h. set up

Above No 46245 *City of London* in British Railways crimson lake livery.
Photo by London Midland Region (B.R.)

Below 6222 *Queen Mary* approaches Crewe with the down 'Coronation Scot' in 1937.
Photo by T. G. Hepburn.

TABLE 2. Down 'Coronation Scot' trial run, 29 June 1937

Locomotive: Cl. 7P 4–6–2 No 6220 *Coronation*
Load: 8 coaches, 263 tons tare, 270 tons gross
Driver: T. J. Clarke; Fireman: J. Lewis

Distance miles		Sched. mins.	Actual m. s.	Speeds m.p.h.
0·0	EUSTON		0 00	—
1·0	mp. 1		2 39	32
3·0	Kilburn		5 29	54
5·4	WILLESDEN JUNC.	8	7 53	68
8·1	Wembley		10 05	76
11·4	Harrow		12 27	79
13·3	Hatch End		14 04	82
17·4	WATFORD JUNC.	18	17 02	86½
20·9	Kings Langley		19 40	82
24·5	Hemel Hemstead		22 20	80½
28·0	Berkhamsted		24 55	80½
31·7	TRING	30	27 45	80½
36·1	Cheddington		30 55	87½
40·2	Leighton Buzzard		33 56	75*
46·7	BLETCHLEY	41	38 57	82
52·4	Wolverton		43 08	86/77½*
54·8	Castlethorpe		44 57	79
59·9	ROADE	51	48 56	76½
62·8	BLISWORTH	53½	51 09	86
69·7	Weedon		56 20	77*
75·3	Welton		60 38	82/78
80·3	Hillmorton		64 23	85
82·6	RUGBY	70	66 28	39*
83·2	Rugby No 7		67 35	38*
88·1	Brinklow		72 20	79
91·4	Shilton		74 47	82
93·5	Bulkington		76 27	79
97·1	NUNEATON	82	79 05	83
102·3	Atherstone		83 08	72*
106·5	Polesworth		86 33	75
110·0	TAMWORTH	94	89 24	77/73*
116·3	LICHFIELD	99	94 25	76½/72
121·0	Armitage		98 10	80½
124·3	RUGELEY	106	100 46	71*
127·2	Colwich		103 20	60*
129·5	Milford		105 29	70½
133·1	Stafford No. 1		108 59	30*
133·6	STAFFORD	115	109 56	30*
136·9	Gt. Bridgeford		113 43	58½
138·9	Norton Bridge	120	115 45	60
143·4	Standon Bridge		119 44	75½
147·6	Whitmore	127	122 48	85
150·1	Madeley		124 27	84½
153·3	Betley Road		126 25	108
156·0	mp. 156		127 53	113
157·0	mp. 157		128 27	—
158·1	CREWE	135	129 46	—

* Permanent speed restriction.

by the LNER on Stoke Bank with Class A4 Pacific No 2509 *Silver Link* on 27 September 1935. A feature of the press run was to be an attack on this record, and no less a person than R. A. Riddles, then a Vice-President of the LMS, was on the footplate. The engine was specially fitted with a Hasler speed recorder in the cab, and was handled by Driver T. J. Clarke and Fireman J. Lewis. In view of their necessarily limited familiarisation with the new engine, their performance, set out in Tables 2 and 4, was very fine indeed.

In the northbound direction, after a brisk start, there was a steady acceleration up 1 in 339 to 82—and the train was still accelerating—and on the subsequent 1 in 335 to Tring a steady 80

TABLE 3. Down 'Coronation Scot' trial run, 29 June 1937

Detailed speeds, Whitmore–Crewe

	Time for half-mile secs.	Average Speed m.p.h.
Whitmore		
mp. 148		
mp. 148½	20·8	86·5
mp. 149	20·4	88·2
mp. 149½	19·8	90·9
mp. 150	19·2	93·6
Madeley		
mp. 150½	19·0	94·5
mp. 151	18·6	96·8
mp. 151½	18·2	98·9
mp. 152	17·8	102·3
mp. 152½	17·4	103·4
mp. 153	17·4	105·9
Betley Road		
mp. 153½	16·8	107·1
mp. 154	16·6	108·4
mp. 154½	16·4	109·8
mp. 155	16·2	111·1
mp. 155½	16·0	112·5
mp. 156	16·0	112·5
Basford sand		
Sidings		
mp. 157	steam off	
Crewe		

was maintained for 7 miles. I estimate the equivalent D.B.H.P.'s at 1,535 and 1,470 respectively, based on post-war resistance tests with BR standard stock. 'Even time' from Euston was thus achieved by Bushey, and Rugby was passed in the remarkable time of 66 min. 28 sec., without any higher speed than 87½ m.p.h. With the train comfortably ahead of time the running now was a little more restrained—in fact, the downhill work was being done on an easy rein, probably with a long-term view to the maximum effort required for the attempt on the speed record between Whitmore and Crewe.

At this time the junction at Stafford No. 1 had not been realigned, and the recovery was from 30 m.p.h. It was not until Norton Bridge, passed at 60, that *Coronation* was opened out. 8·7 miles uphill to Whitmore, at 1 in 509/650/590/398, produced an acceleration to 85, requiring something like 1,600 equivalent D.B.H.P., and then the engine was put hard at it on the down grade with no easing at all. Indeed, speeds suggest that the acceleration down the 1 in 177 to Madeley did not satisfy those on the footplate and the engine was worked still harder from Madeley on the flatter grades to get the desired result. This is no prolonged racing ground like the descent from Stoke Summit.

Recorders on the train, on the basis of the successive half-mile timings shown in Table 3, gave credit for a maximum speed of 113 m.p.h., but the LMS claimed 114 m.p.h. on the evidence of the Hasler recorder chart taken from the locomotive; in retrospect it seems a somewhat brave claim, but it was generally accepted at the time.

But this haste brought a near-brush with disaster in slowing for the Crewe stop, for maximum speed had not been achieved until little over 2 miles from Crewe station and the braking distance had been under-estimated on the footplate. The engine hit the 20 m.p.h. reverse curve at Crewe South into platform 3 at 52 m.p.h. By great good fortune the train was not derailed, but the violent lurch

TABLE 4. Up 'Coronation Scot' trial run, 29 June 1937

Locomotive: Cl. 7P 4–6–2 No 6220 *Coronation*
Load: 8 coaches, 263 tons tare, 270 tons gross
Driver: T. J. Clarke; Fireman: J. Lewis (Crewe N)

Dist. miles		Sched. mins.	Actual m. s.	Speeds m.p.h.	Dist. miles		Sched. mins.	Actual m. s.	Speeds m.p.h.
0·0	CREWE	0	0 00	—	79·9	Kilsby Tunnel N.		63 35	75
1·1	mp. 157		2 23	—	82·8	Welton		65 46	86
4·8	Betley Road		6 06	71½	88·4	Weedon		69 41	92/79*
3·0	Madeley		8 44	74	95·3	BLISWORTH	82	74 24	92
10·5	Whitmore	11	10 42	80½	98·2	ROADE	84	76 22	88½
14·7	Standon Bridge		13 32	90	103·3	Castlethorpe		79 36	100
19·2	Norton Bridge	18	16 51	74*	108·7	Wolverton	88½	81 08	83*
21·2	Great Bridgeford		18 25	82	111·4	BLETCHLEY	93	85 10	89
24·5	STAFFORD	23	20 58	—	117·9	Leighton Buzzard		89 32	93/85*
25·0	Stafford No. 1		21 45	30*	122·0	Cheddington		92 21	89/87
28·6	Milford		25 13	75	126·4	TRING	107	95 23	86½
30·9	Colwich		27 05	80/71*	130·1	Berkhamsted		97 59	90/85*
33·8	RUGELEY	31	29 18	90	133·6	Hemel Hemstead		100 16	93
37·1	Armitage		31 02	88	137·2	Kings Langley		102 30	99
41·8	LICHFIELD	37	34 44	—	140·7	WATFORD JUNC.	117½	104 53	84*
44·6	Hademore		36 36	92/89	144·8	Hatch End		107 45	85
48·1	TAMWORTH	42	38 55	90	146·7	Harrow		109 00	96
51·6	Polesworth		41 27	78*	150·0	Wembley		111 05	95
55·8	Atherstone		44 41	83/71*	152·7	WILLESDEN JUNC.	127	112 50	85*
61·0	NUNEATON	54	48 29	90	155·1	Kilburn		114 33	79*
64·6	Bulkington		50 58	86	157·1	mp. 1		116 57	—
66·7	Shilton		52 29	98½	158·1	EUSTON	135	119 00	—
70·0	Brinklow		54 42	85*					
74·9	Rugby No. 7		58 25	88½/40*					
75·5	RUGBY	66	59 27	40*					
77·8	Hillmorton		61 51	67½					

* permanent speed restriction.
Average speed, Crewe–Euston 79·7 m.p.h.

cleared the dining car of crockery. A good 'hush-up' job was done—indeed, the true story was not revealed to the public until R. A. Riddles referred to it in his Presidential Address to the Junior Institution of Engineers in December 1947—and one can now smile cynically at the comment of Cecil J. Allen at the time that:

"though we certainly took the first crossover at a higher than normal speed, the excellence of the track layout brought us through these reverse curves into the platform with no worse casualties than a few unexpected embraces of passengers preparing to alight?"[1]

But it was the return journey which was to provide the real excitement in the performance field, and the opening minutes, with the train only 12 seconds outside 'even time' passing Whitmore, were a precursor of what was to follow. The acceleration from $71\frac{1}{2}$ to 74 m.p.h. up the three miles of 1 in 177 to Madeley required some 1,820 E.D.B.H.P., while the '90' mark was reached or passed no less than 6 times before Rugby, despite intermediate speed restrictions. Acceleration was lively—witness from 40 passing Rugby to 75 at Kilsby Tunnel North up 1 in 202/370—and the downhill running was sufficiently unrestrained to produce six more 'nineties' and a maximum of just 100 m.p.h. at Castlethorpe. I do not know whether Fireman Lewis dipped his scoop in Castlethorpe troughs, but if he did it would have taken some fetching out afterwards!

Thus the 158·1 miles from Crewe to Euston were reeled off, unchecked, in precisely 119 minutes, at an average speed of 79·7 m.p.h. start-to-stop, while over the 67·2 miles from Welton to Wembley the average was no less than 87·0 m.p.h. A noteworthy send-off to a new service indeed.

TABLE 5. Down 'Coronation Scot: 1.30 p.m. Euston–Glasgow

Locomotive: Cl.7P 4–6–2 No 6220 *Coronation*
Load: 9 coaches, 297 tons tare, 310 tons gross
Driver not stated

Dist. miles		Sched. mins.	Actual m s	Speeds m.p.h.
0·0	CARLISLE	0	0 00	—
4·1	Rockcliffe		5 42	
8·6	Gretna Junc.		9 33	75/65*
13·0	Kirkpatrick		13 29	70
16·7	Kirtlebridge		16 34	$81\frac{1}{2}$
20·1	Ecclefechan		19 08	—
	Castlemilk		—	75
25·8	LOCKERBIE	23	23 52	$77\frac{1}{2}$
			p.w.s.	
28·7	Nethercleugh		27 13	—
34·5	Wamphray		31 45	$85\frac{1}{2}$
39·7	BEATTOCK	35	35 38	$75\frac{1}{2}$
42·3	Auchencastle		37 53	$55\frac{1}{2}$
45·4	Greskine		41 42	$42\frac{1}{2}$
47·8	Harthope		45 20	37
49·7	Beattock Summit	50	48 29	$39\frac{1}{2}$
52·6	Elvanfoot		51 21	—
57·8	Abington		55 47	—
63·2	Lamington		59 46	85
66·9	Symington	65	62 44	—
73·5	CARSTAIRS	71	69 12	—
			sig. stop	
89·4	MOTHERWELL	88	90 54	—
			p.w.s.	
95·7	Newton	95	97 20	—
			sig. stop	
102·3	GLASGOW CEN.	105	110 59	—
			Net time 101 mins.	

* Permanent speed restriction.

In day-to-day running on the 'Coronation Scot', however, such displays of power were quite unnecessary, and 1,250 E.D.B.H.P. was normally adequate south of Carlisle with the 9-coach formation of this train, allowing 68–70 to be sustained on the long stretches of 1 in 335 (or thereabouts) climbing. These were, of course, the days of the single chimneys on the 'Duchesses', and their steaming limit would undoubtedly be somewhat lower than was later afforded by the double chimneys.

The run tabulated in Table 5, on the Down 'Coronation Scot' north of Carlisle shows the rather harder work called for on that section. It is very clear that the driver, whose name was not recorded, had evolved something very akin to working at a constant steam rate, for his uphill work to Beattock Summit—which Cecil J. Allen was justified in describing at the time as "superlative"[2]—produced 1,720 E.D.B.H.P. on the 1 in 200 past Kirkpatrick, 1,795 by a sustained 75 m.p.h. on the 1 in 200 up to Castlemilk, and 1,740 on the last stages of Beattock bank, when a minimum of 37 m.p.h. at Harthope was followed

Above 'Princess Royal' class No 46209 *Princess Beatrice* arrives at Crewe with the down 'The Royal Scot'. Waiting to take the train on is No 46221 *Queen Elizabeth*.
Photo by Douglas Doherty.

Below No 46236 *City of Bradford* ready to leave Paddington during the 1948 Exchanges.
Photo by F. R. Hebron.

by an acceleration to $39\frac{1}{2}$ on the 1 in 74/77 before Summit. After sprightly running through the upper Clyde valley, and passing Carstairs nearly 2 minutes to the good, the remainder of the run was ruined by checks.

The 'Duchess of Abercorn' trials

It was in February 1939 that a 'Duchess' was really put to the test of its ultimate power potential. The 'Royal Scot' was now running on a 7-hour schedule over the 401·1 miles between Euston and Glasgow: it loaded heavily, and the 'Princesses' were showing signs of distress with loadings over 550 tons. The operating authorities wanted to establish whether these, now proved, engines could work still heavier trains on these timings, perhaps permitting some amalgamation of services.

The engine selected was No 6234 *Duchess of Abercorn*, and at 8.10 a.m. on Sunday, 12 February she started out from Crewe with a 20 coach train, including dynamometer car, on the 7 hour timings to Glasgow. On this day she had the standard single chimney.

Overall performance was by no means good and point-to-point times were not kept. Steaming under these hard conditions was unreliable, the dynamometer car summary on the main gradients showing pressures of between 202 and 220 lb between Carnforth and Shap Summit, 220–230 lb from Motherwell to Beattock Summit and 200 lb between Plumpton and Shap Summit. The Polmadie men who took over the down train at Carlisle did not really get the measure of what was expected of them for some time, and the report says that:

"between Carlisle and Beattock Station 9·4 minutes were lost by the engine due, mainly, to the in-different steaming of the en-gine, the management of the fire not being up to the required standard."

Despite this, good economy was achieved, with an overall coal consumption figure of 3·08 lb/D.B.H.P./hr.

The engine was now put specially into Crewe Works to be fitted with a double blastpipe and chimney of simple design, and on 26 February the test was repeated under similar conditions. The running on both days is set out in Table 6 (Down) and Table 7 (Up): those for the 12th are cut short at Motherwell because the train suffered diversion via Bellshill for permanent way work, and for the down double-chimney run on the 26th it was started from Winsford Junction, because of a disastrous start with single line working between Minshull Vernon and that point. The engine on the second day was in the competent hands of Driver G. Garrett and Fireman S. Farringdon, from Crewe North Shed, between Crewe and Carlisle, while a different Polmadie crew worked the train in each direction between Carlisle and Glasgow.

The official report of the trials does not give details of speeds, but for the major climbs charts of speed and D.B.H.P. against distance are given, and this information for the double-chimney runs is reproduced in Figs. 1 and 2 (Down) and Figs 3 and 4 (Up). It should be mentioned that the D.B.H.P.'s shown on these charts do not always reflect the maxima shown in tables in the report.

Fig. 1 and the report show that between Carnforth and Grayrigg, Garrett started at 25% cutoff for the climb to Yealand, probably pulled up to 20% before Burton, was down to 25% by Hincaster Junction and left the controls unaltered not only to the summit, but also on the easy gradients to Dillicar troughs. Boiler pressure was being maintained at 245–250 lb sq. in. and he was clearly going to take Shap by storm! On the bank he used a maximum of 35% cutoff, and it would appear he settled on 30% as soon as he hit the 1 in 75, probably 33% by Scout Green and the final 35% a mile or so beyond. Pressure did not fall below 240 lb at the top. For some 33 minutes, Fireman Farringdon had been providing steam for 1,750–2,000 D.B.H.P. (not corrected for engine weight on the banks) at a rate of about 34,000 lb/hr, the engine consuming some 2 tons of coal per hour.

Driver Marshall clearly did more adjusting of his reverser north of Carlisle, between the limits of 20% and 25% before Beattock, and kept up a rather steadier D.B.H.P. in the 1,600–1,800 range. But approaching Beattock he must have 'dropped her down' to 30% and about 35% by Auchencastle, with 40% reserved for the stretch above Harthope. 245 lb pressure was being maintained rock steady: the drop in D.B.H.P. between Auchencastle and Greskine is not explained in the report, but it may be that Marshall sensed a slip in the offing and briefly eased.

The return journey produced some exceedingly fine hill climbing. From Motherwell up to Craigenhill (Fig. 3), D.B.H.P.'s of 1,900–2,000 were being exerted to sustain speeds of 43–44 on the 1 in 100 grades, cutoffs being in the 30–35% range with the boiler pressure steady at 250 lb/sq. in., indicative of some very competent shovel work by Fireman Smith of Polmadie. In getting away from the Carstairs slack, the engine was not unduly pressed, but after reaching 65 in the Lamington dip, Driver McLean began progressively to pile on the effort, until from Crawford to Beattock Summit the engine was producing over 2,200 h.p. at the drawbar. Again cutoffs of 30–35% were

Right Backing down to Central station having come off Polmadie M.P.D. is No 46223 *Princess Alice.* 24/7/59.
Photo by Douglas Doherty.

Below No 46250 *City of Lichfield* in final British Railways green livery and 2nd style emblem.
Photo by London Midland Region (B.R.)

TABLE 6. Dynamometer Car Tests: Crewe–Glasgow

Locomotive: Cl.7P 4–6–2 No 6234 *Duchess of Abercorn*
Load: 20 coaches, 604 tons tare. 607 tons gross

Date Blastpipe		12 February 1939 Single			26 February 1939 Double			
Driver Fireman		Crewe N men to Carlisle, Polmadie men forward			G. Garrett } Crewe to S. Farringdon } Carlisle		J. Marshall } Carlisle to D. Lynn } Glasgow	
Dist. miles		Sched. mins	Actual m s	Remarks	Sched. mins	Actual m s	Speeds m.p.h.	Remarks
0·0	CREWE	0	0 00					
2·7	Coppenhall Junc.	5	sigs 6 35		passing Winsford Junc. dead slow due to permanent way work and single line working			
8·7	Winsford Junc.	11	sigs 15 05		0*	0 00	—	
16·2	Weaver Junc.	18	22 20		7	7 10		
24·0	WARRINGTON	25	30 10		14	14 05		
27·5	Winwick Junc.	29	33 35		18	17 30		
35·8	WIGAN	38	sigs 44 00		27	25 20		
39·1	Standish Junc.	42	p.w.s. 49 10		31	29 50		
45·55	Euxton Junc.	49	56 10		38	36 20		
50·9	PRESTON	55	61 40		44	42 15		
52·2	Oxheys	58	65 00		47	46 10		
60·4	Garstang	66	73 20		55	54 30		
71·9	LANCASTER	76	sigs 84 35		65	sigs 64 45		
78·2	CARNFORTH	81	91 20		70	70 35	75/67	
91·0	OXENHOLME	95	105 55	1348 max. D.B.H.P.	84	82 00	75/41	2120 max. D.B.H.P.
104·1	TEBAY	111	122 55	1720 max. D.B.H.P.	100	96 50	75	1934 max. D.B.H.P.
109·6	Shap Summit	120	132 30	1620 max. D.B.H.P.	109	103 55	30	2065 max. D.B.H.P.
123·1	PENRITH	133	144 15		122	115 30		
127·9	Plumpton	137	148 40		126	120 00		
141·0	CARLISLE	150	160 40		139	132 00		
8·6	Gretna Junc.	11	12 20		11	10 40	53/67	
25·8	LOCKERBIE	28	33 50		28	28 10	57/80	1733 max. D.B.H.P.
39·7	BEATTOCK	41	50 25		41/43	39 40†	60	1823 max. D.B.H.P.
10·0	Beattock Summit	20	20 05	Assisted in rear	61	56 10	30	2081 max. D.B.H.P.
27·2	SYMINGTON	35	36 10		76	74 00 78 25		Special water stop
33·8	CARSTAIRS	42	42 20		83	86 40		
44·3	Law Junc.	53	53 20		94	97 20		
49·7	MOTHERWELL	60	58 50		100	103 20		
54·2	Uddingston	Thence diverted			104	106 50		
56·0	Newton	via Bellshill			108	110 25		
58·6	Rutherglen Junc.				112	113 25		
62·6	GLASGOW CEN.				118	118 25		

* Passing time.
† Water stop omitted.

TABLE 7. Dynamometer Car Tests: Glasgow–Crewe

Locomotive: Cl. 4–6–2 No 6234 *Duchess of Abercorn*
Load: 20 coaches. 604 tons tare, 607 tons gross

Date Blastpipe Driver Fireman		12 February 1939 Single Crewe N men forward. Polmadie men to Carlisle			26 February 1939 Double N. McLean } Glasgow to G. Garrett } Carlisle to A. Smith } Carlisle S. Farringdon } Crewe			
Dist. miles		Sched. mins.	Actual m s	Remarks	Sched. mins.	Actual m s	Speeds m.p.h.	Remarks
0·0	GLASGOW CEN.		Diverted via Bellshill		0	0 00		
12·9	MOTHERWELL	0 pass	0 00		19	19 45		
18·3	Law Junc.	10	8 05	1682 max. D.B.H.P.	29	26 40	43/47	1.998 max. D.B.H.P.
28·8	CARSTAIRS	34	23 25	1,545 max. D.B.H.P.	43	39 30	44/25*	1.978 max. D.B.H.P.
35·4	Symington	32	32 15		51	48 15	57/50	1.638 max. D.B.H.P.
39·1	Lamington		—			52 08	65	
44·5	Abington		—			57 13	62	
47·0	Crawford		—	2.163 max. D.B.H.P.		59 36	65	2.282 max. D.B.H.P.
49·7	Elvanfoot		—			62 03	63/68	
52·6	Beattock Summit	50	48 50		69	64 40	63	
62·6	BEATTOCK	60	57 05		79	73 35		
76·5	LOCKERBIE	72	67 25		91	84 25		
93·7	Gretna Junc.	87	80 40		106	97 45		
102·3	CARLISLE	97	90 55		116	106 30		
4·9	Wreay					8 59	42	
7·4	Southwaite					11 52	63	
10·8	Calthwaite			1,935 max. D.B.H.P.		15 11	64	2.511 max. D.B.H.P.
13·1	Plumpton	19	19 40	1,650 max. D.B.H.P.		17 45 sigs.	71	2.394 max. D.B.H.P.
17·9	PENRITH	24	24 50	1,595 max. D.B.H.P.		21 50	69/73 53*	2.331 max. D.B.H.P. or 1 in 125
31·4	Shap Summit	43	45 15			40 15	38	
36·9	TEBAY	48	51 50			44 40		
42·9	Grayrigg		—			50 23		
50·0	OXENHOLME	60	62 45			56 30		
62·8	CARNFORTH	71	73 05			67 00		
69·1	LANCASTER	76	78 35			72 20		
80·6	Garstang	87	89 55			84 00		
88·8	Oxheys	94	97 10			—		
90·1	PRESTON	97	99 45			93 35		
95·5	Euxton Junc.	104	108 00			—		
99·4	Coppull		—			105 53		
101·9	Standish Junc.	112	114 35			—		
105·2	WIGAN	116	118 55 sig. stop			113 05		
113·5	Winwick Junc.	124	132 55			—		
117·0	WARRINGTON	128	136 40			126 10 sigs.		
124·8	Weaver Junc.	136	145 15			134 25		
132·3	Winsford Junc.	142	152 05			—		
138·3	Coppenhall Junc.	148	157 15			153 05		
141·0	CREWE	153	162 00					

* Water stop omitted.

Figure 1

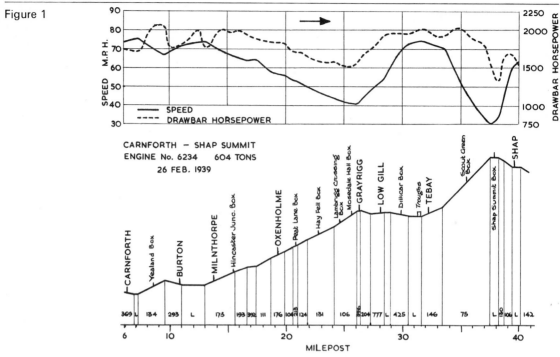

Figure 2

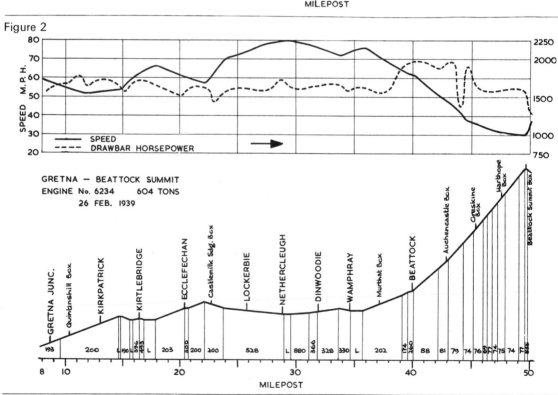

Figure 3

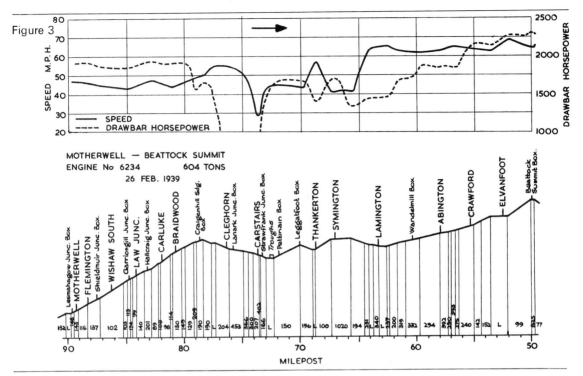

MOTHERWELL — BEATTOCK SUMMIT
ENGINE No 6234   604 TONS
          26 FEB. 1939

Figure 4

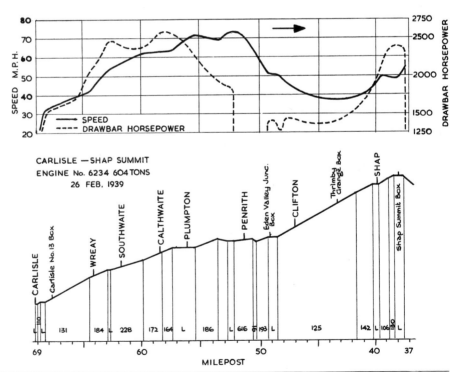

CARLISLE — SHAP SUMMIT
ENGINE No. 6234 604 TONS
        26 FEB. 1939

No 46247 *City of Liverpool* running into Carlisle with the down 'The Royal Scot'. 27/8/60. *Photo by Douglas Doherty.*

being used, with boiler pressure maintained at 245 lb/sq. in.; the equivalent D.B.H.P., allowing for the weight of the engine on the grade, must have been of the order of 2,600, and the steam rate about 39,000 lb/hr.

So early was the train at Carlisle that a lengthy wait ensued to be sure of getting the road, and from the restart a tremendous attack was made on the climb to Plumpton, with a maximum D.B.H.P. (not equivalent) in excess of 2,500 at one stage. Again cut-offs of 30–35% were used, with pressure gradually falling to 230 lb/sq. in. before shutting off for adverse signals through Penrith. This check seems to have caused considerable caution on the climb from Eden Valley Junction, for it was not until after Thrimby Grange that D.B.H.P. exceeded 1.400: a final effort, using 40% cutoff, produced a rapid acceleration on

the 1 in 142 and subsequent easier grades. Shap Summit was passed in $40\frac{1}{4}$ minutes from the Carlisle start, but unchecked and on the form previously displayed this would not have exceeded 37 minutes. The running forward to Crewe was very restrained, and Driver Garrett was content to spin out his point-to-point times from Carnforth onwards to adhere closely to the timetable.

Coal consumption (excluding lighting up) for this massive effort was fairly heavy at 68·7 lb/mile, but the specific consumption of 3·12 1b/D.B.H.P./hr shows good economy. The combustion rate of 75·7 lb/sq. ft grate/hr was quite modest, and showed the extent to which the boiler, now well draughted, was master of its job. The unsensational wording of the dynamometer car report fairly exudes an atmosphere of quiet satisfaction.

Wartime

Unlike the East Coast main line, where wartime conditions tied enormous trains on to the tails of Pacifics and V2's, the LMS operators normally kept their express trains down to about 17–18 coaches, and the easy schedules caused the 'Duchesses' few problems. I recall, however, travelling to Scotland in the summer of 1942 and the train being stopped by signal at Scout Green box, right on the 1 in 75, despite a most cautious approach. The 'Duchess' was unable to lift the train away, partly because of the driver's anxiety about catchpoints— curiously enough, the engine did not even slip during his efforts— and it was necessary to call up a banker from Tebay: total delay was no more than 20 minutes.

But given the opportunity and the will, some fine performances were turned out, as the run in Table 8 confirms. This was made on the 10.0 a.m. Euston–Glasgow Central in 1942,[3] with a 16-coach train of 525 tons gross, and a special stop at Preston was the spur to the driver (whose name was not recorded) to start by attaining 74 on the level past Galgate. The climb to Grayrigg was notable for a sustained $43\frac{1}{2}$ m.p.h. on the 1 in 131 to Lambrigg Crossing, requiring nearly 1,800 E.D.B.H.P., and speed fell no lower than 37 at the top after 2 miles of 1 in 106.

Shap was attacked at 67, and surmounted at 30 in just over 8 minutes from Tebay. This was prewar performance with a vengeance.

A quite incredible performance on the same train in 1944 attracted no attention until 15 years later, when Mr. O. S. Nock published details[4] of a climb of Grayrigg bank by No 6244 *King George VI*. The train had been stopped at Sedgwick intermediate block signals, but a superlative effort was made from the restart. Table 9

details the acceleration on the bank, and compares the speeds with the theoretical figures based on a steady 40,000 lb/hr steam rate under similar conditions. It will be seen that, to mp. 21, this rate was not being achieved, but thereafter the engine was opened right out to a steam rate appreciably in excess of this figure; in the process she was probably being worked at about 45% cutoff. Mr. Nock estimated that the engine was producing about 2600 E.D.B.H.P. in the latter stages of the climb, thus amply demonstrating the capacity of the steam locomotive to produce, for short periods, tremendous power output by mortgaging the boiler water level and, perhaps, pressure.

The 1948 Interchange Trials

It is right that it should be mentioned that No 46236 *City of Bradford* took part in these trials in comparison with a 'King', an A4, a 'Merchant Navy' and a 'Royal Scot'. Beyond that it hardly seems necessary to elaborate. The running of all engines for much of the time showed post-war lassitude to a marked degree, and the task imposed (e.g. 500 tons at 'limited load' timings between Euston and Carlisle) would hardly have taxed any of the engines, even if attempts had been made to keep time. In practice, a combination of inadequate briefing of drivers, inadequate experience on 'foreign' routes, easy tasks and, on some routes, a multiplicity of engineering and signal slacks combined to give a most dismal overall picture, only illuminated by some of the 'Merchant Navy' work and a few flashes of brilliance from the 'Royal Scot'. For the 'Duchess' it did no more than establish—if it were needed—that its specific fuel consumption under such conditions was comparable with what *Duchess of Abercorn* had done in 1939.

TABLE 8. Wartime 10.0 a.m. Euston–Glasgow (1942)

Locomotive: Cl. 7P 4–6–2 No 6221 *Queen Elizabeth*
Load: 16 coaches, 480 tons tare, 525 tons gross
Driver not stated

Dist. miles		Sched. mins	Actual m s	Speeds m.p.h.
0·0	PRESTON	0	0 00	—
1·3	Oxheys	3	5 18	—
4·8	Barton		10 09	—
	Brock		—	68
9·5	Garstang	13	14 34	—
	Scorton		—	$71\frac{1}{2}$
15·3	Bay Horse		19 36	—
	Galgate		—	74
19·9	Lancaster No. 1		23 34	*
21·0	LANCASTER	26	24 27	—
24·1	Hest Bank		27 19	64
27·3	CARNFORTH	33	30 15	69
	mp. $19\frac{1}{2}$		—	$53\frac{1}{2}$
31·8	Burton and Holme		34 46	—
34·6	Milnthorpe		37 19	67
	Hincaster Junc.		—	$55\frac{1}{2}$
40·1	OXENHOLME	50	43 23	$49\frac{1}{2}$
43·6	Hay Fell		47 58	
	Lambrigg Crossing		—	$43\frac{1}{2}$ steady
47·2	Grayrigg		53 18	37
53·2	TEBAY	69	59 41	67
56·2	Scout Green		63 14	41
58·7	Shap Summit	81	67 54	30
60·7	Shap		70 29	—
68·0	Clifton		76 46	79/60*
72·2	PENRITH	96	80 51	55*
77·0	Plumpton	101	85 31 sigs.	$70\frac{1}{2}$
	Calthwaite		—	severe
82·7	Southwaite		93 43	
88·7	Carlisle No. 13		100 00	
90·1	CARLISLE	116	102 42	
			Net time $98\frac{1}{2}$ mins.	

* Permanent speed restriction.

The Results of Scientific Testing

If one looks at the published information about 'Duchess' performance—and I have analysed in some detail well over 100 such performances—it soon becomes apparent that, *Duchess of Abercorn* apart, the standard in the '50s reached a level far higher than anything seen before the war. It seems appropriate, therefore, to an understanding of such running to look at the results of the full series of tests, at the Rugby Testing Station and subsequently on the Skipton–Carlisle line, carried out with engine No 46225 *Duchess of Gloucester* during 1957 and 1958. These tests produced the highest power output from a steam locomotive which has been seen in this country.

On the plant, the locomotive was tested with the 'standard' coals, Grade 1A South Kirkby 'Barnsley Hards' and Grade 2B Blidworth 'Top Hards', and a speed range from 20 to 90 m.p.h. was fully covered. On the road, only the Grade 1A coal was used, and practical operating difficulties limited the speed range to 20–80 m.p.h.

Steaming rates with the live steam injector were pushed to a maximum of 41,500 lb/hr on the plant and 40,000 lb/hr on the road. The report says that:

"considerable difficulty was caused by slipping at high power outputs, both on the test plant and on the line, and the maximum steaming rate and maximum power developed were limited by this factor."

No front end limit was established for South Kirkby coal, but it was 'certainly appreciably above' the sustained rate of 41,500 lb/hr with the existing draughting. The drawbar tractive effort/speed curves are partly reproduced in Fig. 5.

As an indication of further difficulties in producing high power

TABLE 9. 10.5 a.m. Euston–Glasgow Central (1944)
Locomotive: C1.7P 4–6–2 No 6244 *King George VI*
Load not recorded

	Actual Speed	Calculated speed at 40,000 lb/hr steam rate	Corresponding cutoff
Sedgewick I.B. sig.	0	0	–
OXENHOLME	29½	30	49
mp. 21	43	46½	38
mp. 22½	54	50	36
mp. 24½	60	52½	35
mp. 25½	56	53	34
Grayrigg	55	53	34

Figure 5

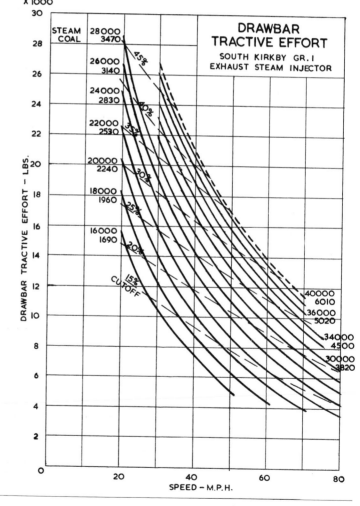

Above In early British Railways days, livery experiments were made. No 46238 *City of Carlisle* is here shown in blue livery and first style emblem.
Photo by London Midland Region (B.R.)

Below No 46236 *City of Bradford* at Clifton Road Junction, Rugby, with a Euston—Blackpool express. Coming off the Peterborough line is No 58218 with a freight train. 23/4/59.
Photo by Douglas Doherty.

outputs, the report states that the upper limits of output were set:

"... mainly by the liability to slipping but also, on the line, by the limited water capacity of the tender ... and the difficulty of handling bagged coal at a sufficient rate in the confined space of a coal bunker..."

in the special tender used. Bear in mind that coal was being fired at a rate of one ton every 22 minutes!

Apart from the slipping problem, there were a few minor troubles. Blowing of cylinder relief valves was a persistent one, as also was the tendency for the safety valves to blow off light (thus confirming my own experience that 250 lb valves gradually deteriorated to blow at about 235 lb/sq. in. both on 'Duchesses' and on 'Scots'). It was necessary, too, to reset the piston valves to given even work at both ends of the cylinders, since the standard Crewe setting produced appreciably lower M.E.P.'s. at the back end.

As to the economy, an absolute minimum specific steam rate of 14·16 lb/I.H.P./hr was established at a high steaming rate, but at more normal rates a figure of 14·5 lb/I.H.P./hr was more typical. This was a little higher than with the 'King', 'Britannia' and V2, the difference being attributed to the large piston valves and generous clearance volume (12·5%) of the 'Duchess'. It was also affected by the modest superheat, the steam temperature not exceeding 700°F until a steam rate of about 37,000 lb/hr was reached in spite of the 40–element supheater with high surface area.

This latter feature, perhaps surprising to the uninitiated, was caused by poor design ratios for the superheater flues, the *A/S* ratio being 1/550. As a result, the gas temperature at exit from the flues was some 50°F *lower* than that of the superheated steam

Figure 6

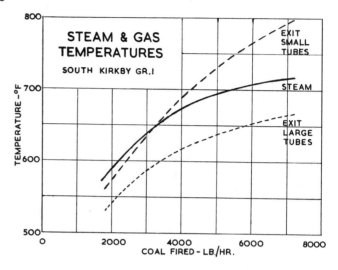

TABLE 10. Locomotive Test Run: Carlisle–Skipton
Locomotive: Cl.8P 4–6–2 No 46225 *Duchess of Gloucester*
Load: 442 tons tare, including dynamometer car and mobile test units working, equivalent load 900 tons approx.
Driver not stated

Dist. miles		Actual Time m s	Speeds m.p.h.
0·0	Cumwhinton	0 00	—
2·9	Cotehill	5 54	30 min.
6·1	Armathwaite	11 12	—
	Slipping in Armathwaite and Barons Wood Tunnels		
11·3	LAZONBY	17 21	70
14·4	Little Salkeld	19 53	74
	Langwathby	—	55
19·5	Culgaith	25 00	60
		p.w.s.	30
24·0	Long Marton	29 45	—
26·9	APPLEBY	34 50	—
29·3	Ormside	37 46	54
	Slipping in Helm Tunnel		
34·4	Crosby Garrett	46 00	37
37·6	Kirkby Stephen	52 06	31½
	Mallerstang	—	30
			sustained on 1 in 100

Constant steam rate: 40,000 lb/hr.

Above No 6202 Turbomotive on shed at Edge Hill M.P.D. in September 1936.
Photo by W. Potter.

Below Carlisle, 7.40 a.m. No 46231 *Duchess of Atholl* is imminent for departure with a Euston–Glasgow sleeper. 18/7/59.
Photo by Douglas Doherty.

TABLE 11. Down 'Midday Scot': 1.15 p.m. Euston–Glasgow

Locomotive: Class 8P 4–6–2 No 46255 *City of Hereford*
Load: to Carlisle—16 coaches, 510 tons tare, 545 tons gross
       forward   —14 coaches, 447 tons tare, 480 tons gross

Driver not recorded Crewe North

Dist. miles		Sched. mins.	Actual m s	Speeds m.p.h.	B.P.	Reg.	Cutoff
0·0	CREWE	0	0 00	—	215	FV	45
						Full	25
2·8	Coppenhall Junc.	5	6 33	54	230	,,	20
	Minshull Vernon		8 39	65	,,	,,	
8·8	Winsford Junc.	11	12 10	71	,,	,,	,,
11·9	Hartford		14 40	76/74	220	,,	16
	Acton Bridge		16 48	75	200	,,	20
16·3	Weaver Junc.	18	18 17	65	—	Shut	—
22·1	Acton Grange Junc.	25	24 06	66	200	F/FV	25
			sigs.			Shut	—
24·1	WARRINGTON	27	26 48	25	215	FV	25
			then sigs and p.w.s. to				
45·5	Euxton Junc.	62	63 05	67	—	FV	35
	Leyland		64 31	70	235	Shut	—
51·0	PRESTON	69	69 13	21	—	FV	50
			sigs.				
52·3	Oxheys	72	72 49	21	—	FV	35
			sigs. to				
60·5	Garstang	80	86 14	54	200	Full	15/20
66·3	Bay Horse		92 21	68	200	,,	20
	Lancaster No. 1		96 45	67/60*	210	FV	25
72·0	LANCASTER	91	97 46	69	,,	½	,,
75·1	Hest Bank		100 28	73	,,	Shut	—
			sigs.				
78·2	CARNFORTH	97	105 56	5	235	FV	50
			easy start to				
82·7	Burton		115 13	47	215	Full	15
85·5	Milnthorpe		118 23	56	—	,,	,,
87·4	Hincaster Junc.		120 39	45/47	215	,,	20
			sigs.				
91·1	OXENHOLME	112	128 34	2	225	Full	28/32
	Hay Fell I.B.		—	34	,,	,,	32
96·3	Lambrigg Crossing		139 56	36	215	,,	,,
98·2	Grayrigg		143 04	36	210	,,	25/22
104·1	TEBAY	129	149 15	68	215	Full	22/25/30
	Scout Green		152 27	49	,,	,,	32/35
	Shap Wells I.B.		—	35	—	,,	40/50
			slip			FV/F	60/70
109·5	Shap Summit	139	156 42	34/31	200	FV	55
111·7	Shap		159 29	—	205	Shut	—
120·0	Eden Valley Junc.		166 28	81	—	—	—
123·2	PENRITH	152	169 21	53*	235	Full	25/30
128·1	Plumpton	157	174 07	77	170	FV	25
133·77	Southwaite		178 35	80/78	—	Shut	—
139·7	Carlisle No. 13		183 14	—			
141·0	CARLISLE	a 171	186 14	—			
0·0		d 0	0 00	—	220	½	35
2·0	Kingmoor		4 13	48	220	Full	30/25/22
4·1	Rockcliffe		6 19	64	225	,,	18
	Floriston		8 03	74	,,	,,	,,
8·6	GRETNA JUNC.	11	10 01	75	,,	,,	20
12·9	Kirkpatrick		13 58	66/63	220	,,	25/20
16·6	Kirtlebridge		17 19	74	,,	,,	25

Dist. miles		Sched. mins.	Actual m s	Speeds m.p.h.	B.P.	Reg.	Cutoff
20·0	Ecclefechan		20 06	69	,,	,,	..
25·7	LOCKERBIE	29	24, 57	66/73	,,	½	..
28·6	Nethercleugh		27 19	75	215	Full	20
31·6	Dinwoodie		29 48	72	,,	,,	22
34·4	Wamphray		32 07	77	210	,,	20
39·6	BEATTOCK	42	37 31	—			
			42 58†		220	Full	25/35/40
45·4	Greskine		52 55	43	200	,,	40
	Harthope I.B.		p.w.s.	18		Full	35
49·6	Beattock Summit	62	61 19	36		Full/FV	30
55·2	Crawford		66 36	64	—	Shut	—
			p.w.s.				
57·7	Abington		69 28	22	—	Full	20
63·1	Lamington		75 35	69	200	FV/Full	23/25
66·8	Symington	78	78 45	67	—	Shut	—
	Leggatfoot		81 30	72/65	—	FV	25
			sigs.				
73·1	Strawfrank Junc.		84 46	74/25		Shut	—
73·5	CARSTAIRS	86	86 05	—			

* Permanent speed restriction.
† Banked in rear by ex CR O–4–4T.
Water consumption: Crewe–Carstairs 9,300 gallons = 43·3 gallons/mile.

(Fig. 6); in other words, in the last few feet of the flues the steam was actually being *cooled* by the flue gases. Indeed, the report tantalisingly refers to the fact that:

"in 1938 the header and last few feet of the elements of one of these engines were lagged, with a resulting increase in superheat of 20–30°F."

The lowest specific coal consumption was 1·835 lb/I.H.P./hr with South Kirkby coal and live steam injector, this figure coming down to 1·70 lb/I.H.P./hr with the exhaust steam injector in use: this injector, however, could not deliver more than 32,500 lb/hr. Tests on the line established a 'low' of 15·93 lb water/D.B.H.P./hr and 1·995 lb coal/D.B.H.P./hr with the exhaust steam injector.

Just what such high rates of working mean in practical terms may be judged by the test performance southbound from Carlisle at 40,000 lb/hr steam rate, set out in Table 10, with a load

simulated at 900 tons by the mobile test units linked to the dynamometer car. The coal rate averaged 118 lb/mile! More of this theme later.

The Fifties: 'Duchesses' Come into Their Own

I have deliberately discussed the results of the testing programme out of chronological order, because the knowledge imparted by them is useful for a proper appreciation of the work done by the 'Duchesses' during the '50s. After the easement of wartime restrictions, a number of years was devoted to rehabilitation of permanent way on the West Coast main line, overcoming arrears of locomotive and rolling stock maintenance, and building new BR standard coaches. Then, in the early fifties the 'Special Limit' and 'XL Limit' timings began to reappear in the working timetables, and some of the work expected of the big Pacifics was

very exacting indeed. Nor did they fail to rise to the occasion.

In May 1953 I had occasion to travel to Glasgow en route to Wester Ross, and joined a pair of highly competent Crewe North men on the footplate of No 46255 *City of Hereford* at Crewe to work the down 'Midday Scot'. It was the Friday before Whitsun, and there was a relief in front of us which had not been running particularly well south of Crewe. By the time we got away, with a full train of 16 coaches grossing 545 tons, we were 17 minutes late. Table 11 gives details of the running.

The engine was not pressed at the start, for the driver wisely waited to see the sort of path he was going to get. But the 'Royal Scot' on the relief seemed to be showing a clean pair of heels, and so we made a fair run past Weaver Junction, only to be pulled up short by signals at Walton New Junction. This heralded a slow passage through industrial

Lancashire, with a further signal check and three permanent way slacks. Even so, we kept the easy sectional time to Preston, only to get signals on again at Oxheys box due to a Windermere train being put down in front of the relief. We got away very gently on successive single and double yellows until the greens reappeared at Garstang, and then made a sprightly getaway, only to be brought almost to a stand at Carnforth while the relief, no doubt heavily checked by the Windermere train, hammered up the 1 in 134 to clear Yealand I.B. signals.

Again, discretion was demonstrably the better part of valour, and we got away modestly, without exerting the engine in any way. The driver was mentally calculating the line occupation ahead, and obviously had visions of the Windermere again delaying the relief at Oxenholme before clearing on to the branch. Sure enough we got the backwash of it, and we crawled up Oxenholme platform, brakes released and a breath of steam on, waiting for the starter to clear. If he had been so minded, the driver could have got off and felt his outside big end while we drifted.

33½ late, we got the road, and *City of Hereford* was put at the bank, with nothing between her and Carlisle—we hoped; 225 lb on the clock, (10 lb under blowing off pressure), regulator up against the stop, cutoff at 28%, quickly advanced to 32%, and she was really making what the Americans used to call 'stack music'. By the time we cleared Lambrigg Crossing, at the end of the 1 in 124/131, speed was up to 36 m.p.h., and on the 2 miles of 1 in 106 from there to Grayrigg she held this speed with an E.D.B.H.P. of 1,750. Steam rate to do this was about 30,000 lb/hr—not high, but the boiler had had no chance to settle down to any steady steaming until now. There

was no pausing for breath past Low Gill, of course—pressure was at 215 lb, water level well up—and with full regulator and 22–20% cutoff Shap was going to be rushed!

We hit the 1 in 146 beyond Dillicar troughs, having picked up 1,750 gallons of water, at 68, and now we saw a demonstration of how to use the characteristics of the steam locomotive to assault the bank by using the capacity of the boiler as a reservoir as well as a steam producer. Cutoff was immediately lengthened to 25%, and to 30% as we came on to the 1 in 75. By Scout Green, still doing 49, it had been increased in stages to 35%, and soon after it went down further to 40%. By Shap Wells I.B. signal it was lengthened again to 50% at 35 m.p.h. and *City of Hereford* was making wonderful sounds indeed. I think the driver would then have left her thus, had she not hit a bad patch of rail and slipped.

But the driver was ready for just that, and fairly pounced on the regulator handle, quickly silencing the slip. Immediately he was opening up again, dropping down to 60% and that little bit more even torque, and as she took it, gradually opened up further, getting his shoulder under the regulator handle until it was fully open again. Then, as a final gesture of defiance for the last ¼ mile, the reverser went round again to the 70% mark, and *City of Hereford* had it all! The signalman at Shap Summit box must have been used to noise, but seldom can they have heard anything like our approach! We cleared the bank at 31, with pressure down to 200 lb and water at about half glass before we levelled off, and I reckon that the locomotive had been turning out little short of 1,800 E.D.B.H.P. in the process. The time of 28m 8s from a crawl at Oxenholme to Shap Summit was only a minute over the booked allowance, while from Tebay to Summit the 7m 27s time

showed a 2½ minute gain. The fireman could now sit down for 20 minutes and have a wash and his tea.

At Carlisle we dropped two coaches from our tail and set off (after station overtime) 35½ minutes late. Mossband troughs were known to be empty for repairs, but the tender had been topped right up at the Carlisle column, for the next troughs were 72 miles away, with some heavy climbing in between. This was always the weakest link in the water chain on the West Coast, and any uncertainty meant an almost inevitable stop at Beattock Station tank.

The published runs behind 'Duchesses', so far as I can trace, only show one run (apart from those with the lightweight 'Coronation Scot' and post-war 'Caledonian' trains) which equates the passing time at Wamphrey on this occasion, and that with only 11 coaches. 'Even time' was bettered by Lockerbie, with minimum speeds on the 1 in 200 of 63 above Kirkpatrick and 66 before Castlemilk, achieved on 25% cutoff with full regulator, and involving 1,970–2,070 equivalent D.B.H.P.

But by this time water was down to 2,250 gallons in the tender, and with the 10 miles of 1 in 75 of Beattock Bank and 22 miles beyond that to Pettinain and replenishment, it was just a little chancy to go through. Being wise after the event, we should have reached the troughs with about 700–800 gallons in hand, but drivers can hardly be expected to calculate with that accuracy while running a heavy train at speed. So we drew up for a partial fill at Beattock station in the remarkable time, for 39·7 miles from Carlisle, of 37m 30s start-to-stop.

The Caley 0–4–4T on duty as banker took an unconscionable time buffering up at the rear end, but once we set off he must have wondered whether his journey was

Above No 46240 *City of Coventry* in red livery on Willesden M.P.D. 8/3/64.
Photo by W. Potter.

Below Rainy day at Crewe North M.P.D. No 46228 *Duchess of Rutland* in red livery. 24/9/61.
Photo by W. Potter.

really necessary. Before the permanent way slack over Harthope viaduct, the train had been worked up to 43 m.p.h. on grades averaging 1 in 75, with *City of Hereford* shouting to the pine forests at 40% cutoff with full regulator. I do not know whether there was daylight showing between the buffers of the banker and the last coach—such things *have* been known!—but I calculate that the total equivalent D.B.H.P. was at least 2,750, of which it is a safe bet that the Duchess was producing at least 2,100. So, despite the 18 m.p.h. slack on the bank, we passed Summit in 18m 21s from the standing start.

On to Carstairs the running was not particularly exciting, and we just kept overall time from Carlisle, notwithstanding $5\frac{1}{2}$ minutes stationary at Beattock and two permanent way slacks. Had our driver not stopped for water, we could have cut the 86 minute timing to $77\frac{1}{2}$ minutes, or 73 minutes net allowing for the Harthope and Abington slowings—only 2 minutes over the prewar 'Coronation Scot' timing but with 150 tons more train. Overall, it had been an unsatisfying run, but reflecting very fine enginemanship all the same. The overall water consumption of 43·3 gallons/mile was commensurate with the high power outputs achieved, and would be equivalent to about 57 lb of coal per mile.

Now I would like to turn to performance on some of the hardest turns which 'Duchesses' were called upon to hold down in the '50s, and here I quote from articles in the *Railway Magazine* and *Trains Illustrated* of the time. One such job was the 'Midday Scot' in both directions, always a heavily loaded train and running, in 1954, on an overall timing of 8 hours 15 minutes between Glasgow and Euston, with six intermediate stops.

Table 12 sets out the Carstairs–Carlisle–Lancaster portion of a

TABLE 12. Up 'Midday Scot': 1.30 p.m. Glasgow–Euston (Limited load)
Locomotive: Class 8P 4–6–2 No 46233 *Duchesses of Sutherland*
Load: 14 coaches, 453 tons tare, 495 tons gross
Driver: Latham, Fireman: A. Clarke (Crewe N)

Dist. miles		Sched. mins.	Actual m s	Speeds m.p.h.
0·0	CARSTAIRS	0	0 00	—
3·5	Leggatfoot		6 17	39/63
6·6	Symington	9	9 58	49
10·3	Lamington		13 24	80
			p.w.s.	20
15·7	Abington		20 57	62
18·2	Crawford		23 24	64/59
20·9	Elvanfoot		26 07	$65\frac{1}{2}$
23·8	Beattock Summit	28	29 07	52
28·1	Greskine		32 57	80/72*
33·8	BEATTOCK	38	37 29	82
			p.w.s.	35
39·0	Wamphray		42 5&	60
44·8	Nethercleugh		48 15	74
47·7	LOCKERBIE	50	50 45	$69\frac{1}{2}$
50·8	Castlemilk		53 33	
53·4	Ecclefechan		55 46	74
56·8	Kirtlebridge		58 20	85/77
60·5	Kirkpatrick		61 10	$80\frac{1}{2}$
64·9	GRETNA JUNC.	65	64 51	70
69·6	Rockcliffe		69 00	65
			sigs.	
73·5	CARLISLE	75	77 45	—
1·4	Carlisle No. 13		3 49	36
4·9	Wreay		9 06	46
7·0	Southwaite		11 40	$60\frac{1}{2}$
10·7	Calthwaite		15 28	60/56
12·8	Plumpton	21	17 50	64
17·9	PENRITH	27	22 47	60/71
21·1	Eden Valley Junc.		25 52	62
22·6	mp. $46\frac{1}{2}$		27 24	53
23·6	mp. $45\frac{1}{2}$		28 36	49
24·6	mp. $44\frac{1}{2}$		29 54	$45\frac{1}{2}$
25·6	mp. $43\frac{1}{2}$		31 15	44
26·6	mp. $42\frac{1}{2}$		32 38	$43\frac{1}{2}$
27·6	mp. $41\frac{1}{2}$		34 01	$43\frac{1}{2}$
28·6	mp. $40\frac{1}{2}$		35 23	44
29·4	Shap		36 24	49
31·4	Shap Summit	48	39 02	45
36·9	TEBAY	54	44 06	85/70*
			sigs.	20
42·9	Grayrigg		51 37	45
50·0	OXENHOLME	66	58 30	78/70*
55·5	Milnthorpe		63 00	$77\frac{1}{2}$
59·6	mp. $9\frac{1}{2}$		66 23	67
62·8	CARNFORTH	78	68 55	86
66·0	Hest Bank		71 14	84
69·1	LANCASTER	85	74 39	—

* Permanent speed restriction.

fine run with a 14 coach train of 495 tons gross,[5] which typifies sound, steady enginemanship with none of the 'starve-and-burst' attitude that one often saw. The first notable feature was the energetic recovery, on the rising grades of upper Clydesdale, from the permanent way slack at Wandelmill, to 64 in the five miles to Crawford, and after 59 before and 65½ after Elvanfoot, to fall no lower than to 52 on the 2 miles of 1 in 99 to Beattock Summit. The calculated E.D.B.H.P. on this section was fully 1,885. Again, the gentle rise from Nethercleugh to Castlemilk, carried at a minimum of 67, saw excellent work.

Similar standards prevailed on the climb to Shap Summit; 46 at Wreay, a sustained 60 on the 1 in 228 past Southwaite, maintained as high as 56 up 2½ miles of 1 in 172/164, was good going with this load. On the long drag past Thrimby Grange, on the 1 in 125, speed settled at 43¾ m.p.h., and the whole climb to Shap showed E.D.B.H.P's in the 1,780–1,940 range. (Note the consistency with the Beattock climb.) Driver Latham and Fireman Clarke could be proud of their work, with net times of 69 minutes for the 73.5 miles to Carlisle and 72 minutes for the 69.1 miles on to Lancaster.

Another exacting job was invariably the last sleeping car train from Euston to Glasgow, routed via the G. & S.W. line and attaching (or rather, inserting) a restaurant car for breakfasts at Carlisle. The loading was invariably over 500 tons tare, and could exceed 550 tons. Table 13 details one of the most remarkable performances recorded with this train,[6] under the incentive of a late start from Carlisle, in the last years of the 'Duchesses' on express passenger work.

The first climb extends almost continuously to Carronbridge, including 4½ miles at 1 in 200 past Auldgirth and 7 miles, mainly at

1 in 150, from Closeburn to Carronbridge. This was run entirely at between 53 and 63 m.p.h., and required some 2,170 E.D.B.H.P. Cecil J. Allen rightly described this as 'outstanding'. That power of this order could be sustained for 21 minutes—a steam rate of 37,000 lb/hr and coal rate of about 5,250 lb/hr are the measure of it—with little easing beyond, indicates firemanship of the very highest order, and it is unfortunate that individual credit cannot be given. The second climb to Upper Cairn I.B. signals was spoilt by a permanent way check, and a second slack in the vicinity of New Cumnock troughs may well have caused the crew some anxiety. Necessarily restrained running on the curves prevented any high speed before Garrochburn, but the quick 79 before the Hurlford slowing was a nice touch.

The formidable climb out of Kilmarnock to the summit at mp. 17, before Dunlop, was also tackled in the same exuberant style. In falling no more than from 40 to 38 up nearly 1½ miles of 1 in 87 to mp. 20, some 2,190 equivalent

TABLE 13. Down sleeping car express: Euston–Glasgow

Locomotive: Class 8P 4–6–2 No 46249 *City of Bradford*
Load: 14 coaches, 532 tons tare, 555 tons gross
Driver not stated

Dist. miles		Sched. mins.	Actual m s	Speeds m.p.h.
0·0	DUMFRIES	0	0 00	—
3·4	Holywood		6 06	53/58½
7·5	Auldgirth		10 23	54/60½
11·45	Closeburn		14 12	63
14·15	Thornhill	18	16 56	57½
17·5	Carronbridge		20 34	53/64½
26·1	Sanquhar	33	29 18	51
29·45	Kirkconnel		33 10	—
			p.w.s.	35
32·3	mp. 59½		37 40	41/62
			p.w.s.	40
36·9	New Cumnock	46	43 30	46
42·25	Cumnock		50 14	59
44·25	Auchinleck		52 10	65
48·65	Mauchline	57	56 08	67
51·4	Garrochburn	2†	58 35	70/79
56·3	Hurlford		62 51	60*
58·05	KILMARNOCK	70	65 36	—
2·25	Kilmaurs		4 28	40
3·7	mp. 20		7 45	38/41
5·5	Stewarton		10 18	42
6·7	mp. 17		12 16	36
10·0	Lugton Junc.	17	16 05	58/70
14·7	Neilston Low		20 12	51*
16·8	BARRHEAD	25	22 07	—
			sigs.	20/24
21·95	Crossmyloof	3†	32 25	39
24·15	ST. ENOCH	40	38 03	—

Net times: Dumfries–Kilmarnock   61½ mins.
          Kilmarnock–St. Enoch   33 mins.
* Permanent speed restriction.   † Recovery time

D.B.H.P. was being exerted, and this standard of performance was continued to the top.

Yet another train where the fireman led no life of slippered ease was the 7.55 a.m. out of Euston, a combined Liverpool and Manchester business express, calling at Watford to pick up and then non-stop to Crewe on 'XL Limit' timings. 16 coaches was the normal order of the day, hard up against the limit of 510 tons, and the working could not have been in more capable and reliable hands than those of Edge Hill top link men. In another book[7] I have written in glowing terms of the work of the late Maurice Corbett and his regular fireman at that time, Stan Walls, and the run in Table 14 is by another pair from the same link, Driver Aitchison and Fireman Corfield, with *Duchess of Hamilton* and a 16 coach train grossing 535 tons.[8]

Note the sustained 64 m.p.h. up the 1 in 335 to Tring from the Watford start, which would require 25% cutoff for a steam rate of 32,000 lb/hr and 4,200 lb of coal per hour, giving some 1,800 E.D.B.H.P. The steam rate was not much lower on the level stretches, and brisk running along the Trent Valley line had won back the loss from three permanent way slacks by Stafford. But then, with nose to home, followed a tremendous effort on the rising grades to Whitmore, including an acceleration from $71\frac{1}{2}$ at Standon Bridge, up nearly 3 miles of 1 in 398, to no less than $74\frac{1}{2}$ at Whitmore. This must have needed 30% cutoff and a steam rate in excess of 40,000 lb/hr, for just over 2,200 E.D.B.H.P. was involved. How deplorable that such worthy endeavour should be nullified by a signal stop outside Crewe. The net time of 125 minutes represents a start-to-stop average of 67.5 m.p.h.—with 535 tons! To conclude this survey, I revert to the 'Midday Scot' in 1958, running on 'XL Limit' timings and,

in the run set out in Table 15[9] overloaded by 15 tons for a 'Duchess'. Not that such a triviality had any deterrent effect on Driver H. Nicklin or Fireman Roberts from Crewe North shed, for they kept or bettered booked times in spite of two permanent way checks. The bank from Wembley to Carpenders Park was not taken hard, almost as though the enginemen were getting *Princess Alexandra*

into her stride by degrees, but the climb to Tring produced 1,960 E.D.B.H.P. as a foretaste of what was to come.

There were two more highlights before Rugby. On the rise to Roade, mostly at 1 in 326/330, speed was held at a steady 72 m.p.h. with this very big train, requiring no less than 2,340 E.D.B.H.P. The steam rate must have been in excess of 42,000 lb/hr, but so little was the

TABLE 14. 7.55 a.m. Euston–Liverpool/Manchester

Locomotive: Class 8P 4–6–2 No 46229 *Duchess of Hamilton*
Load: 16 coaches, 500 tons tare, 535 tons gross
Driver: Aitchison;   Fireman: Corfield (Edge Hill)

Dist. miles		Sched. miles	Actual m s	Speeds m.p.h.
0·0	WATFORD JUNC.	0	0 00	—
3·5	Kings Langley		5 58	57
7·1	Hemel Hempstead		9 34	62
10·6	Berkhamstead		12 52	64
14·3	TRING	16	16 20	64/73
			p.w.s.	47
18·7	Cheddington		20 20	—
22·8	Leighton Buzzard		24 16	71
29·3	BLETCHLEY	28	29 40	74
35·0	Wolverton		34 17	78
42·5	ROADE	39	40 45	62
45·4	BLISWORTH	42	43 25	$71\frac{1}{2}$
52·3	Weedon	48	49 06	$73\frac{1}{2}$
59·9	Welton		54 02	$64\frac{1}{2}$
			p.w.s.	37
65·2	RUGBY	60	62 47	32*
70·7	Brinklow		69 03	64
76·1	Bulkington		73 57	70/76
			p.w.s.	15
79·7	NUNEATON	74	78 48	56
84·9	Atherstone		83 58	66
89·1	Polesworth		87 28	$76\frac{1}{2}$
92·6	TAMWORTH	87	30 12	80
98·9	LICHFIELD	93	95 07	$68\frac{1}{2}$
103·6	Armitage		99 15	73
106·9	RUGELEY	100	101 53	$76\frac{1}{2}$
112·1	Milford	105	106 10	70
116·2	STAFFORD	110	110 01	54*
121·5	Norton Bridge	116	115 02	$66\frac{1}{2}$
126·0	Standon Bridge		119 01	$71\frac{1}{2}$
130·3	Whitmore	125	122 36	$74\frac{1}{2}$
132·8	Madeley		124 35	79
135·9	Betley Road		126 54	86
			sig. stop	
140·7	CREWE	136	136 43	—

Net time 125 mins.

* Permanent speed restriction.

engine winded by this effort that speed was worked up to no less than 88 on the level to Weedon, itself requiring something of the order of 2,200 D.B.H.P. Thus, for something like 20 minutes, until steam was shut off for Rugby, Clarke was having to fire at a rate of about 3 tons an hour, placing coal with precision and attending to all his other duties at the same time. The remainder of the journey to Crewe was excellent, with a first class climb to Whitmore, but it had no need to rise to the same standard as before. The pinnacle of firemanship produced remarkable results with a 'Duchess', no less than with other engines, but there are limits which not even Fireman Clarke could be expected to better for long.

The 'Duchesses' as They Might Have Been

Our tale so far has, I hope, drawn a picture of an extremely able locomotive, limited only by the skill and two-handed endurance of the fireman—just as, in the ultimate, was the 'Britannia', 'Royal Scot' or even Class 5. The big boiler could enable miracles to be sustained for brief periods, but in the end it was the sweating man with the knotted handkerchief on his head and the shovel in his hands who could not stand the pace. The official **BR** assessment of the fireman's capability was, of course, 3,000 lbs of coal per hour. We have seen examples of engines using steam at a rate of 40,000 lb/hour or more, but unless 6,000 lb of coal per hour could be conveyed to the right place on the grate the boiler had to be mortgaged and before long nature foreclosed. There was, of course, only one real answer if the full potential of the engine were to be realised—a mechanical stoker.

If this is accepted, then a number of corollaries became evident:

(i) greater coal capacity would be required if through workings between London and Glasgow or Crewe and Perth were to continue

(ii) greater water capacity would be required to bridge that Mossband–Pettinain gap *reliably*

(iii) the ashpan design had to cater for increased ash production

(iv) the brick arch would require improved support for the higher duty imposed on it

(v) the superheater required redesign to improve gas flow and steam temperatures

(vi) the boiler feed arrangements would require 'beefing-up'

(vii) at prolonged high-speed high output the inside big ends,

TABLE 15. Down 'Midday Scot'': Euston–Glasgow
Locomotive: Class 8P 4–6–2 No 46224 *Princess Alexandra*
Load: 16 coaches. 525 tons, 570 tons gross
Driver: H. Nicklin: Fireman: Roberts (Crewe North)

Dist miles		Sched mins	Actual m s	Speeds m.p.h.
0·0	EUSTON	0	0 00	—
			Banked to Camden No. 1	
5·4	WILLESDEN JUNC.	9	10 45	56
8·1	Wembley		13 30	56
11·4	Harrow		16 53	61
13·3	Hatch End		18 52	57
17·4	WATFORD JUNC.	21	22 45	72
20·9	Kings Langley		26 00	64
24·5	Hemel Hempstead		29 10	65
28·0	Berkhamsted		32 20	63
31·7	TRING	35	35 45	67
36·1	Cheddington		39 15	82/84
40·2	Leighton Buzzard		42 21	78
			p.w.s.	36
46·7	BLETCHLEY	47	49 10	48
52·4	Wolverton		54 54	72
54·8	Castlethorpe		56 51	72
59·9	ROADE	58	61 05	72
62·8	BLISWORTH	61	63 30	81
69·7	Weedon	67	68 27	88
76·6	Kilsby Tunnel S		73 50	74/80
82·6	RUGBY	80	80 00	—
14·5	NUNEATON	15	16 00	80
19·7	Atherstone		19 55	72*
23·9	Polesworth		23 15	80
27·4	TAMWORTH	28	25 54	74
33·7	LICHFIELD	34	31 10	64
38·4	Armitage		35 30	72
41·7	RUGELEY	41	38 30	72
44·6	Colwich		41 01	64
46·9	Milford	46	43 10	64
51·0	STAFFORD	51	47 15	56*
56·3	Norton Bridge	57	53 07	56
60·8	Standon Bridge		57 38	64
65·0	Whitmore	66	61 35	64/66
			p.w.s.	28
70·7	Betley Road		68 50	52
75·5	CREWE	77	75 00	—

Net times: Euston–Rugby 77 mins.   * Permanent speed restriction.
          Rugby–Crewe   72 mins.

FIG. 7.   THE "DUCHESSES" AS THEY

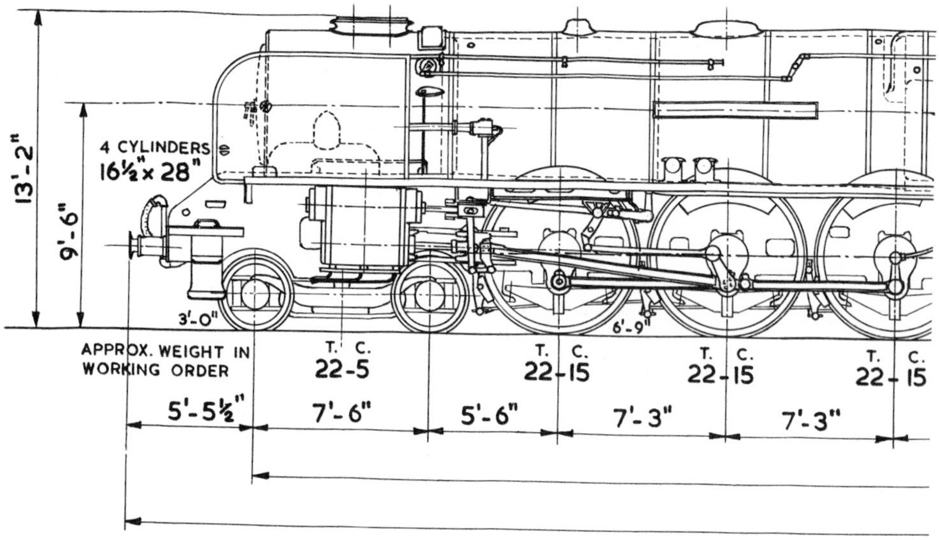

13'-2"
9'-6"

4 CYLINDERS
16½" x 28"

3'-0"

6'-9"

APPROX. WEIGHT IN
WORKING ORDER

	T. C.		T. C.		T. C.		T. C.
	22-5		22-15		22-15		22-15

5'-5½"   7'-6"   5'-6"   7'-3"   7'-3"

TUBE PROPORTIONS:	ORIGINAL	REBUILT
TUBES:		
LARGE	40 5⅛" OD. x 7 SWG.	40 5½" OD. x 7 SWG
SMALL	129 2⅜" OD. x 11 SWG.	134 2⅜" OD. x 11 SWG
SUPERHEATER ELEMENTS	40 TRIPLE, 1" OD. x 11 SWG.	40 RETURN LOOP, 1⅜" OD. x 11 SWG
FREE GAS AREAS:		
LARGE TUBES	3·66 SQ. FT.	4·05 SQ. FT.
SMALL TUBES	3·23 SQ. FT.	3·45 SQ. FT.
TOTAL	6·89 SQ. FT.	7·50 SQ. FT.
A/S RATIOS:		
LARGE TUBES	1/540	1/499
SMALL TUBES	1/431	1/431

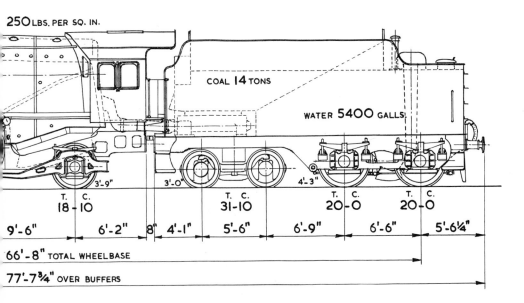

GHT HAVE BEEN. DRAWN BY JOHN POWELL.

250 LBS. PER SQ. IN.

COAL 14 TONS

WATER 5400 GALLS.

3'-9"   3'-0"   4'-3"

T. C.   T. C.   T. C.   T. C.
18-10   31-10   20-0   20-0

9'-6"   6'-2"   8" 4'-1"   5'-6"   6'-9"   6'-6"   5'-6¼"

66'-8" TOTAL WHEELBASE

77'-7¾" OVER BUFFERS

HEATING SURFACES:	ORIGINAL	REBUILT
TUBES	2577 SQ.FT.	2713 SQ.FT.
FIREBOX	230 SQ.FT.	230 SQ.FT.
ARCH TUBES	-	18 SQ.FT.
TOTAL EVAPORATIVE	2807 SQ.FT.	2961 SQ.FT.
SUPERHEATER	830 SQ.FT.	761 SQ.FT.
TOTAL	3637 SQ.FT.	3722 SQ FT.
GRATE AREA	50 SQ.FT.	50 SQ.FT.
FREE GAS AREA AS PERCENTAGE OF GRATE AREA	13·8%	15·0%
TRACTIVE EFFORT (85% B.P.)	39943 LBS.	
ADHESION FACTOR	3·82	

D

excellent as they were, might well have shown distress

(viii) the regulator required re-design to give finer control.

In addition, various mechanical features required improvement to prevent loss of availability from the silly little defects that were the bane of the mechanical firemen—blocked sanding gear, leaking top feed clackbox joints and so on.

I have therefore amused myself by acting as C.M.E. for a day, and given my orders for bringing the 'Duchesses' into a form in which they could have competed on rather more equal terms with the diesels. Fig. 7 shows what the resulting animal might have looked like, and the dimensions that would have applied.

The main changes are:

—the superheater flue size increased to $5\frac{1}{2}$ in. od. to improve the A/S ratios and free gas areas, and thus increase

steam temperatures. Curiously, this can be done without detriment to the number of small tubes.

—provision of three arch tubes in the firebox. Thermic syphons, and the maintenance problems they could be expected to bring in a copper firebox, hardly seem justified.

—the back end frames, trailing truck and ashpan altered along the lines of those on 46256/7.

—fitting a mechanical stoker.

—fitting a multiple valve regulator on the superheat side of the header.

—provision of a new 14 ton, 5,400 gallon tender, without coal pusher, running on two rigid axles and a bogie.

—fitting of SKF roller bearing inside big ends.

—provision of a cab with one-piece floor, and a fireiron tunnel in front of it on the right hand platform.

—fitting a vacuum-operated water scoop,

together with minor detailed improvements.

A New Standard of Performance

It is always intriguing, having amused oneself in this way to wonder what new feats such a locomotive might produce. Fortunately, in this case we can predict the outcome with fair accuracy.

The Rugby Testing Station study of the 'Duchesses' failed to establish the boiler limit, which was seen to be 'appreciably above' a steam rate of 41,500 lb/hr. Adhesion was the limiting factor. It would seem not unreasonable to set a steam rate of 34,000 lb/hr as a working figure for timetable purposes,

Below On Crewe Works on 24/9/61 is No 46252 *City of Leicester* in green livery. *Photo by W. Potter.*

giving an appreciable margin of boiler capacity (even with Grade 2 coal) and adhesion for time recovery.

This would require 4,580 lb of coal per hour with hand firing and Grade 1A fuel: stoker firing with suitable graded coal would probably increase this by around 10%, or say to 5,000 lb/hr.

I have now taken the 'XL Limit' loading for a 'Duchess' of 510 tons tare, and applied the Drawbar Tractive Effort characteristics from Fig. 5 to calculate the performance from Euston to Crewe, observing all speed restrictions and allowing a 10 minute 'warm-up' period from starting at only 30,000 lb/hr.

The result is set out as a footplate trip in Table 16, and gives an overall start-to-stop timing of $137\frac{3}{4}$ minutes for the 158·1 miles—and this with 550 tons gross behind! Rounding off and supplementing the in-built recovery power of the locomotive slightly, one could visualise a working time of 140 minutes (5 minutes less than the 270 ton 'Caledonian' was allowed) with the heaviest trains—in other words, a universal minimum standard for the passenger service With prestige trains limited to, say, 300 tons tare, this suggests a timing of about 130 minutes, which would have brought a 6 hour timing to Glasgow within the realms of daily operating practicability.

But look at some of the detailed figures. Our stoker-fired 'Duchess', working at this high steam rate, marginally fails to keep the 'XL Limit' timing up to Tring, which was expected of flesh-and-blood firemen. Something wrong with the time-table there! After Tring, we get a steady gain on this timing to Nuneaton, after which it begins to accrue in handsful due to unevenness and slackness in the point-to-point timings. And no higher speed than $86\frac{1}{4}$ anywhere—indeed, only six incursions into the 80's, some of them very brief.

Nevertheless, it is enough to give an average of 68·9 m.p.h. start-to-stop, which would have made a lot of commercial sense. Many of the uphill speeds—$64\frac{1}{4}$ at Hatch End, 66 at Tring, $70\frac{1}{2}$ at Roade, $71\frac{1}{2}$ above Welton and 69 at Whitmore—have already been demonstrated *and beaten* by the hand-fired engines.

Also, spare a thought for the cutoff figures in the last column.

TABLE 16. Calculated down run: Euston–Crewe

Locomotive: Class 8P 4–6–2 'Duchess' with mechanical stoker

Load: 15 coaches, 510 tons tare, 550 tons gross

Dist. miles		'XL Limit' Sched mins	Calculated Times m s	Speeds m.p.h.	Cut off
0·0	EUSTON	0	0 00	—	70/60/50/45
1·1	Camden No. 1		3 14	25	45/35/32
5·4	WILLESDEN JUNC.	9	8 53	58	30/27/24
8·1	Wembley		—	$62\frac{1}{2}$	26
14·2	mp. $14\frac{1}{2}$		—	$64\frac{1}{2}$	26
17·4	WATFORD JUNC.	21	20 47	69	25
21·0	Kings Langley		—	70	24
24·5	Hemel Hempstead		—	69	25
28·0	Berkhamsted		—	67	25
31·7	TRING	33	33 21	66	25
36·1	Cheddington		—	79	22
40·2	Leighton Buzzard		—	$83\frac{1}{2}$/80*	22
46·7	BLETCHLEY	47	44 45	82/$80\frac{1}{2}$	22
52·4	Wolverton		—	83/80*	22
54·8	Castlethorpe		—	79	23
59·9	ROADE	58	54 48	$70\frac{1}{2}$	24
62·8	BLISWORTH	61	57 16	77	23
69·7	Weedon	67	63 01	78/77/78	23
75·3	Welton		—	$71\frac{1}{2}$	24
80·3	Hillmorton		—	80	—
82·6	RUGBY	79	73 46	45*	—
83·2	Rugby No. 7		—	45*	33/29
88·1	Brinklow		—	65	26
91·4	Shilton		—	69/68	25
97·1	NUNEATON	93	87 15	80/$81\frac{1}{2}$	24/22
102·3	Atherstone		—	$78\frac{1}{2}$/70*	25
106·5	Polesworth		—	75/78	23
110·0	TAMWORTH	106	96 54	80/79/82	22
116·3	LICHFIELD	112	102 17	$79\frac{1}{2}$/74	23
121·0	Armitage		—	79	22
124·3	RUGELEY	119	108 34	78	22
127·2	Colwich		—	76/77	23
129·5	Milford	124	112 45	76/78	23
133·6	STAFFORD	129	116 19	$75\frac{1}{2}$/60*	27
138·9	Norton Bridge	135	121 12	$68\frac{1}{2}$	25
143·4	Standon Bridge		—	70	24
147·6	Whitmore	144	128 38	69	24
150·1	Madeley		—	75	23
153·3	Betley Road		—	$86\frac{1}{2}$	21
	Basford Hall Junc.		—	78	—
158·1	CREWE	155	137 45	—	

* Permanent speed restriction

None of the magic 15% so beloved of enthusiasts—nothing less than 21% anywhere, and much of the work requiring 25% or more with full regulator. This is utilisation of the built-in capacity of the locomotive, without back-breaking labour, to produce a commercially saleable service: a clean break from the Midland Railway's Society for the Prevention of Cruelty to Small Engines.

Finale

I started by declaring my position in relation to Sir William Stanier's magnum opus. I hope that what I have said subsequently has justified my stance. These were big engines, giving big performances in the hands of men big in stature and spirit. Their gait was regal and their voice commanding, as befitted a 'Duchess'. That three of them are preserved for posterity is entirely fitting. May those who gaze at them in the future appreciate their remarkable qualities to the full.

Above The up 'The Royal Scot' leaving Carlisle behind No 46249 *City of Sheffield* on 21/7/59.

Below On the up Rugby through road with the 'The Caledonian' express is 46243 *City of Lancaster,* 1/7/60. *Photos by Douglas Doherty.*

[1] *Railway Magazine*, August 1937.
[2] *Railway Magazine*, January 1941.
[3] Cecil J. Allen, *Railway Magazine*, January, February 1943.
[4] *Railway Magazine*, February 1959.
[5] Cecil J. Allen, *Railway Magazine*, December 1954 and February 1955.
[6] C. J. Allan, *Modern Railways*, December 1962.
[7] *'Royal Scots' of the LMS*, ed. D. Doherty. Ian Allan, 1970.
[8] Cecil J. Allen, *Railway Magazine*, July 1955.
[9] Cecil J. Allen, *Trains Illustrated*, January 1959.

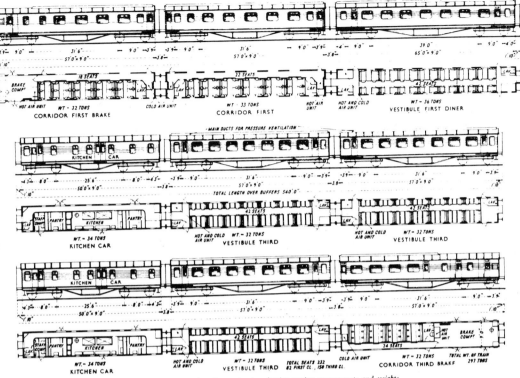

Details of nine-coach make-up of train, *showing seating arrangements and weights*

Details of the make-up of the 'Coronation Scot' train, showing seating arrangements and weights. *Reproduced by courtesy of 'The Railway Gazette'.*

Below No 46247 *City of Liverpool* on up express through Watford on 15/3/61.
Photo by London Midland Region (B.R.)

Above Running non-stop through Rugby with an up express is No 46256 *Sir William A. Stanier, F.R.S.,* named after the Chief Mechanical Engineer of the L.M.S. who was responsible for the design of the 'Duchesses'. 30/8/58.
Below Braking for its Carlisle stop is No 46249 *City of Sheffield* with a Glasgow—Birmingham express. 27/8/60.

The LMS Duchesses—
a driver reminisces

by PETER JOHNSON

I shall for ever remember my first experience on a 'Duchess' class locomotive. It was late 1952, October. I had only the month before been transferred from the ex-GWR shed at Crewe to the ex-LMS North Shed, and had been placed in No. 6 link, the Birmingham link. Other routes were of course worked over in this link, but it was known as the 'Brumijem' link as Birmingham work predominated. However, it was not in the Birmingham area where I found myself on the footplate of No 46256 *Sir William A. Stanier, FRS*, named after the designer of these great locos.

My driver and myself had worked an evening Crewe to Carlisle freight (actually it was my maiden trip to Carlisle, but that is another tale) and we were rostered to 'book off' overnight at Carlisle, a 'double trip' we called it, returning the next day with the 12.50 p.m. Carlisle to London Euston, being relieved at Crewe by Camden men.

After dining in the LM hostel, or 'barracks' at Upperby, Carlisle, me for the first time experiencing the well-known haricot beans for veg. (which I later found out were renowned from Euston to Glasgow) we set about getting ready to book on and prepare the loco., as yet unknown, for our journey Southwards to Crewe.

I remember gazing in awe and reverence at a set of Camden men who were getting ready to leave the barracks at the same time. My driver nodding in acquaintance with them, saying to me "they are the 'Cockneys' for the Scot." The 'Royal Scot'! What a magical sounding name, what schoolboy hasn't heard of the 'Royal Scot'

and here I was in the presence of the driver and fireman who were actually going to work that famous express. These were early days for me, the rest of the firemen in the link taking such happenings as a matter of course, but I was not so used to it as them. Everything to me in those early days was a source of wonderment, fresh ground, and new experience.

Collecting all our belongings from the barracks, my driver and myself made our way to the shed at Upperby, only a stone's throw away really, as the Barracks, in uniform with the majority of hostels, were built very close to the shed premises. Booking on and reporting to the Foreman in charge, he in turn informed us that our loco was all ready and was in the roundhouse. "46256 you have got, a good un."

My mate had told me that we should have a 'Lizzie' going home, so it did not come as a shock that for my first trip from Carlisle I had got a member of such a famous class. All the Stanier Pacifics were nicknamed 'Lizzies' whether they were of the 6200–12 'Princess Royal' class or the 6220–6257 'Princess Coronation' class. Why, I never did find out, everyone I asked gave me a different version. The most common one was that they were all called 'Lizzies' after the famous exploit of No 6201 *Princess Elizabeth* in 1936. Number 6201 was nicknamed 'Lizzie' and I suppose that was to suffice for all the following Pacifics, whether they were the same or not. Anyway my mate said a 'Lizzie' and that was what he referred to them as.

Making my way to the round-house I began to have butterflies.

I had never been on the footplate of a 'Lizzie' before, let alone have to get, and keep steam in one. How I had enjoyed the 'free wheeling' from Shap summit to Carlisle the previous night on my inward journey with the freight, and now we had to climb up that formidable bank, not with a 'slow and easy' freight, but with an express passenger and with an unfamiliar engine too. Well, I had transferred for greater experience, and I had got it.

On arriving at the roundhouse I looked up at the largest piece of machinery I had ever seen. *Sir William A. Stanier FRS* blazed the nameplate proudly displayed on the huge boiler side. Following my mate's example I climbed aboard. I was amazed at the size of the cab, there seemed enough room to ride one's bike around it. I thought to myself 'Blimey' have I got to fire this! I instinctively looked into the firebox. Talk about a firebox, it looked more like a bottomless pit! As yet there was very little fire in it. I had heard several of my new-found mates say, "A Lizzie firebox will hold about three tons of coal," seeing that great void in front of me I could well believe it. Although the engine had been prepared, oiled, examined, etc., the fire had not been levelled all over the box, it was just a 'tump' under the door. A good thing really, as the train fireman can examine the tube-plate for signs of dirty tubes, the corners of the firebox front, or stays as they are called, for signs of water leakage, also the brick arch can be examined for possible loss of bricks, and most important of all, the lead plugs can be examined for possible fusing signs, drops of water dripping from the centre lead core. Should any of these defects be noticed they must be reported at once. When the fire is in a condition like this, the fire bars can be seen which proves that the fire is clean and unclinkered.

The blower was applied, which forces a jet of steam up from the blast pipe in the smoke box into the orifice of the chimney piece, and out to atmosphere, this draws up the fire in the process, preparatory to levelling the fire all over the box. By use of the fire iron I levelled the fire over the box, and started shovelling. After a dozen or so shovels full I looked into the box to see how I was progressing. To my consternation I didn't seem to be getting anywhere, the bars still looked as bare as what they were when I started. The Carlisle preparing fireman was still on the footplate and was rather amused to see my puny efforts at 'filling the box' as he called it. After my driver said "He's a Western man, it's his first trip, never had a 'Lizzie' before", the fireman said, "Here let me show ye how to fill yon box" in his peculiar Cumberland accent. I got out of his way, and watched how he went about it. In these early days of my experience on LMS engines I was grateful for any tips I could get, as on such an engine as a 'Lizzie' my experience was nil. I watched in eager anticipation as the Carlisle man prepared to fill the box. First of all with a shout of "Mind ye feet" he undid the catches which held the tender doors shut. Immediately all the coal which had been behind the doors cascaded down onto the footplate, lumps, cobbles, slack, the lot. When the avalanche of coal had stopped he cleared the doorway and closed and clasped the tender doors. I had never seen so much coal in all my life, it was everywhere. The two drivers and

myself, had, at this fireman's shout "Mind ye feet" lifted them up out of the way. It was a good job, otherwise I'm sure we should all have been buried from the knees downwards. Grabbing hold of the biggest lumps the fireman proceeded to sling them into the firebox, saying, "If they will go through yon hole, they are all reet." Gradually the coal pile was diminished, after all the lumps had gone in the box, the cobbles and slack followed, my assistant using the shovel to get rid of the small stuff. I looked into the firebox expecting to see not a glimmer in there after all this coal had been put on. I needn't have worried, the Carlisle man was experienced and knew what he was doing, the fire was burning nicely and the steam was rising.

Leaving the engine for a moment we placed our claim on the turntable, so as to get off the shed. As we were in the roundhouse, all roads lead fanwise off a centre turntable, and each engine must go to the table to get off the roundhouse. We had to wait, as using the table at the time were the men we had seen in the barracks. No 46244 *King George VI* was their engine, proudly displaying the 'Royal Scot' headboard from the smokebox top lamp iron. I noticed that this engine's tender front was bare of coal and realised that he too had opened the doors, as we had. I found out from the Carlisle man that this operation was a regular done thing, to 'coal the box' as he put it.

Getting the table we made our way up the engine shed yard, filling our tank to capacity before departing from the shed, the fireman giving me some last minute hints on how to 'fire' my strange steed. As we left Upperby shed and made our way, tender first towards Carlisle Citadel Station, the pegs were off on the up line and making her non-stop way, London bound, was No 46244,

her exhaust going sky-high as she lifted the 'Scot' out of Carlisle station. I heard the deep throated beat of the 'Lizzie' as she was put to the climb out of Carlisle station, the whole air seemed to vibrate and pulsate as she pounded past us, her fireman busy shovelling to keep her massive firebox full. What a thrill I experienced as her exhaust beats echoed in the distance as the train passed us by.

My dreamings were abruptly brought to an end as now it was our turn. We had backed on to our train, and I had coupled up. First of all the shackle coupling, screwing it up tight, then steam heating pipes, opening both tender and coach cocks, and last of all the vacuum pipe. Off with the lamp on the tender, a quick look to see that everything was alright, the lamp off the tender on to the front right buffer beam (the other was already on the left) and we were ready. While I was doing this my mate had been putting some coal in the box to be prepared for the long climb up Shap. The guard came and gave us the load, returned to his van and from a wave of his green flag we were away.

Once again I heard the deep throated beat of a 'Lizzie' as we moved our train out of the station, Southwards bound. Seeing that my mate had only just put some coal on, I thought that it would last a bit. How wrong I was. We were hardly out of the station with the train before I noticed that the steam pressure was dropping alarmingly, with a cry from the driver of "Get some on Peter" I started shovelling. To me on this first trip it just seemed like giving a donkey strawberries. I had no sooner got a shovelful of coal in the firehole door when 'Whoosh' it had gone, my task seemed never ending. My mate kept saying "Get some in the back corners." That, at that time was easier said than done. It just wouldn't stay there but was taken down the box with

Passing Upperby M.P.D. Carlisle is No 46245 *City of London* with the up 'The Mid-day Scot'. 25/8/60. *Photo by Douglas Doherty.*

the draught and I just couldn't get it to build up in the back corners at all. I've heard it said since that it's a long drag from Carlisle to Penrith with a green fire. I can vouch for that. It was none so far as on my maiden trip with No 46256. I was very glad to see my mate shut off for the stop at Penrith. The water was in the bottom nut, steam pressure was down to about 180 and the fire was any shape. I'm afraid at that time I didn't reckon much of Stanier Pacifics and was wishing for a more familiar engine, a 'Grange' or a 'Hall', which I was convinced could do the job better than my 'Lizzie'.

All the time we stood at Penrith my driver and myself were filling the firebox. I was up the tender

picking out all the big lumps and he was slinging them in the box regardless of size. We kept it up until we got the right of way again. By this time there was once more a full head of steam, 250 lb, and the water was looking decent in the glass again. Round about the region of (I now know it to be, but didn't then) Thrimby Grange on the climb to Shap, the steam pressure had once again fallen below 200 lb and the water was very low in the glass. With my driver helping me all he could we limped on, and eventually struggled over Shap summit with 140 lb of steam, the water just in sight and the vacuum brakes dragging as we had insufficient steam to blow the brakes off. I couldn't understand this

shortage of steam, as to my way the fire looked in good shape. It was level with the fire hole ring and tapered towards the firebox front, and with it being a wide type firebox I had been firing it at the sides, but something was wrong. I was getting bursts of smoke from the chimney, but she still wouldn't steam.

During the long downhill glide to Lancaster, I got the boiler full up and a full head of steam. Too much in fact, because she started to lift the water from the safety valves and spray everything, us included. Just why there was a division in the cab roof just above the cab seats I shall never know, but when a 'Lizzie' lifted the water from the safety valves, the crew got a steady stream of hot water dribbling straight down their necks. After such a good run through Lancaster the run to Preston was accomplished without much trouble, although the water did come down to half glass, and she didn't blow off.

Leaving Preston, the climb to Coppull again took its toll and we were once again in difficulties. Steam was low, water level was low, vacuum was low, and I was low. I was beginning to wish that I had never transferred. I had heard what a marvellous engine a 'Lizzie' was, and here was I, who had one, and I couldn't get the water hot enough to boil an egg. There was something wrong somewhere and the following week I found out what it was. I will not dwell on my trials in getting from Coppull to Crewe as it was one great tale of woe. Suffice it to say we did eventually arrive, and my driver softened the fireworks when a footplate inspector had a quiet word with me.

The following week after the above episode we were rostered on a Crewe/Carlisle parcel train as far as Warrington, a mere 24 miles. The loco we had got was No 46227 *Duchess of Devonshire*, once again a 'Lizzie'.

Going to the shed road where No 46227 was stabled my driver saw a gang of cleaners. Recognising one he called him over and said "Here, a packet of fags if you show my mate how to get coal in the back corners of a 'Lizzie'." He jumped at the offer and was only too pleased to oblige. On gaining the footplate he immediately set about levelling the fire all over the box, and picking up the shovel he said "Here look, this is how to do it." He proceeded deftly to put a shovelful of coal right into the back corner, the shovel blade being nearly at right angles to the firehole door while doing so. I suddenly realised what had gone wrong the previous week, the back corners

had been completely bare of any fuel, no wonder I was down the nick for steam. Talk about out of the mouths of babes and sucklings. This cleaner had by his simple but very important demonstration, put me on the right footing on how to reach the back corners of a 'Lizzie'. Something else I had learnt, I now knew how to fill the box, and how to reach the back corners. The future looked a bit rosier.

I tried out my new found technique on the *Duchess of Devonshire* and it worked like a charm, I, if anything produced too much steam for so short a journey. I was eager now for another crack at a long distance express.

During that same week I had a chance. We were rostered on one of the overnight sleepers from Glasgow to Euston, picking the train up at Crewe, No 46249 *City of Sheffield* at its head. A set of Crewe men brought it in from Carlisle and we relieved them at Crewe for Euston.

The engine was handed over in tip top condition with the firebox full and the water in the top nut. Getting the tip to leave, away we went, No 46249 threading her way through Crewe South Junction's maze of point work. Clear of the Junction my driver opened out *City of Sheffield* for the climb to Whitmore. Grasping the shovel, eager to try out my new found knowledge, I found it worked like a charm. No difficulty being experienced whatsoever in getting, or maintaining steam. I began to wonder if I was dreaming as I kept testing the level of water in the boiler and examining the steam clock every few seconds. My mate, with a knowledgeable smirk on his face, enquired what was the matter, he hadn't heard me swear once yet. I told him "What a different trip to the previous week," "Ah well", he replied, "Everyone has to learn, this is how they always are" and I found out he was right. When a 'Lizzie' is fired correctly, the

coal being got right back in to the back corners, they are indeed a marvellous engine, but when the back corners are starved as in the case of No 46256, heavy weather can be expected.

I can honestly say that since I was shown by that North shed cleaner just how to get the fuel in the back corners, I was never down the nick again with a 'Lizzie', not through the same fault anyway.

I remember a rough passage from Perth to Crewe in 1954, engine No 46248 *City of Leeds*. The general sort of coal we used to get from Perth, or Glasgow for that matter, was very small, but hot coal. Once there was a good body of fire there it was plain sailing, but took rather a lot to get a body of fire with it being small coal. On this particular trip, the coal was quite a bit larger, about double the size of a pint pot. I was quite pleased about this as it meant I could get a body of fire easier, but my mate in that link (the Perth link Crewe No. 2) was apprehensive, "It's no good" he said "Sooner have the small". It looked alright to me, but still he said it was no good, so according to him we were for it.

We left Perth right on time at 8.15 p.m. with a light train of eight coaches and before we had gone very far I realised my mate had been right, the coal was no good. It seemed to burn brightly, I was firing it right, but it didn't seem to give out much heat as the steam clock testified. I was glad to see the lights of Gleneagles Station that night, our first stop, as things were getting decidedly sticky. I was all for getting the fire irons down and giving it a good poke, but my mate said it wouldn't make any difference, in fact it would make it worse. As I respected his superior judgement I left the fire irons alone. We coaxed her along from Gleneagles to Stirling, and from Stirling up the bank she lagged even with only eight coaches. We had a good blow at Carstairs while three more coaches were attached to our rear, making eleven in all, unknown to me my mate had wired assistance for us from Carlisle onwards.

We left Carstairs and on the short bit of level track to Symington she began to 'jib' again. The long climb to the top of Beattock summit completely winded her and we had to stop for a 'blow up' at Beattock summit box before we dare go any further, even though we had the downward grade of one in seventy five to go down for ten glorious miles. Away we went again filling the boiler to capacity and getting the box full as we proceeded down the bank. By now the glow from the ash pan which we had when we left Perth had gone completely, which proved we had a clinkered fire.

Through Lockerbie and over Gretna and on to Carlisle we went, shutting off when we were able, conserving our water when we could. Arriving in Carlisle the Station Inspector met us and told us that they had got no engine to assist us from Carlisle to Crewe, but could provide assistance to the summit only (Shap) with a tank engine. A 2–6–4T was duly backed on to assist us over the top, the driver informing us that three trains behind us were in difficulties and had all wired assistance from Carlisle. He passed the remark that it was going to be "one of those nights".

Leaving Carlisle we set about the climb to Shap, the staccato bark of the 'tankie' being heard above the restrained beat of our 'Lizzie'. Now that we had assistance we could nurse *City of Leeds* a little, and no undue difficulty was experienced from Carlisle to the summit, as when we got short of steam we just eased up and let the 'tankie' do the work. He left us at the summit with a wave and a hoot on his whistle and we were once again on our own.

We ran to Lancaster and coasted to Preston, by now nearly one hour late. We were hand to mouth from Preston to Coppull but we made it, just. Wigan, our last stop, was arrived at, and I did a thing there to the fire which I have done many a thousand times but never

No 46222 *Queen Mary* on Polmadie M.P.D. during March 1952, shown wearing experimental blue livery. *Photo by W. Potter.*

so surprised as I was then. I dug the shovel blade in the fire, just under the firehole door, intending to lift the top layer of coal up. To my utter astonishment the shovel blade went in a few inches before it reached solid clinker. I reckoned there was at least eighteen inches of solid clinker in the firebox, no wonder she wasn't steaming.

City of Leeds was nursed from Wigan through Warrington and the last bastion, Weaver Junction, steam now being very low. So low in fact that the exhaust injector would not work and we were having to use the live steam one, the large ejector being used to keep the brake off. I could not do anything about it as the fire, or clinker as the case was, was now level with the brick arch. I had my doubts about reaching Crewe at all but my mate said we would make it. We did, just, but when we arrived the fire was out at the front and four inches above the firehole ring at the back and we hadn't got enough steam to ease up to detach ourselves from the train. A Crewe station 'Jinty' had to couple up and ease us up, dragging us to the shed afterwards. It was after this trip that I respected Scottish small coal.

My regular driver in the Perth link was rather a large person standing over six foot and weighing twenty one and a half stone, and seeing as at the time I only weighed eight stone, it was a standing joke with the engine arrangers at Crewe North that they didn't give us the same engine more than twice on the run otherwise it would have to go in for rebalancing of the wheels. I well remember this particular driver for his habit of standing up with his head stuck out of the side window and his rather large backside protruding halfway across the footplate, and seeing that I was a 'wrong side' fireman our backsides used to bump frequently with the oscillation of the footplate. I, being the

far lighter always came off worse, many's the time I've had to pick myself up off the 'deck' with rather a rude exclamation on my lips. My mate looking in complete surprise at my predicament as he had never felt a thing.

Another unfortunate accident happened while I was in the Glasgow link, once again with No 46248 *City of Leeds*. My driver and myself were coaling the box preparatory to working a train to Glasgow. The tender was full of big lumps, and we were both slinging them in, when all of a sudden there was a crash and a bump and the level of the fire in the box dropped about two foot, "Oh Hell" said my mate, "the rocker's gone". So it had, on examination we found out that the whole rocker grate had collapsed and all the fire had gone into the ash pan. The engine had to stand for two days before anyone could get at it and repair it, the pair of us had to see the 'Gaffer' after that.

As I progressed through the links at Crewe North Shed I think I came into contact with nearly every 'Lizzie' which had been built, including the first batch of 'Princess Royals' too. I found these engines, although of a different design, completely capable of working turn about with their counterpart the 'Duchess' class. The only main difference to me as a fireman, being with the exception of No 46206 *Princess Marie Louise*, the 'Princess Royal' class had no steam assisted coal pushers and all coal had to be man handled from the back of the tender when it was needed, and I bet some of it had been there for years and was like concrete.

On being made passed fireman in 1957 I was looking forward to my first Pacific as a driver. It came in the form of No 46246, *City of Manchester* on a Crewe to Glasgow relief to the 'Mid-Day-Scot', rostered to work to Carlisle,

returning the next day with a Glasgow to Euston. I remember the feeling of pride as I prepared my steed. I likened my trip to the first trip I had with *Sir William Stanier*, only this time I was on the other side, and I had no misgivings this time. My fireman was not a 'greenhorn' like I had been, but a regular on the job, in fact only a few years in service behind me. (Actually it was the same fireman who wanted a pint when I tried for the magical 'ton' with No 46139 *The Welch Regiment*)— See 'Royal Scots' of the LMS, published by Ian Allan.

City of Manchester was always considered to be a good loco and on this trip to Carlisle no trouble whatsoever was experienced. That was a 'thing' about the 'Lizzie', provided they were fired correctly and the coal was of average combustion quality they would do everything that was asked of them. There never seemed to be a limit to their capabilities, they always had an ace up their sleeves as it were. I've seen 'Lizzie's' loaded up to the hilt, and they have still kept time. Towards the last they were relegated to the goods work, even on such unglorified work such as this they still gave of their best.

It was with comparative ease with which No 46246 *City of Manchester* lifted her light train of ten coaches, Carlisle bound out of Crewe. In fact the trip was a little monotonous, so little being demanded of loco and crew. In a very short space of time cut off was at 15%, with the regulator what a Western man calls 'on the crack', which is open as little as possible. Warrington and Wigan were passed and very little alteration to the regulator was required to climb past Boars Head and Standish Junction. We coasted down the bank to Preston and across the comparative level stretch through Lancaster to Carnforth, the very start of the big climb to Shap summit. On this trip it didn't

No 6222 *Queen Mary* near Brinklow in 1937 hauling the down 'Coronation Scot' express.
Photo by T. G. Hepburn.

seem to make any difference at all. I opened the regulator half way which opened the first regulator valve fully, and No 46246 leapt up the first bank like a two year old. Until this time my fireman had not even lifted the fire hole door flap, let alone partly shut the doors, and there had been ample steam. Seeing that we were now climbing he did at this stage lift the flap. *City of Manchester* responded by starting to blow off on the 'first valve', I should perhaps explain here that a 'Lizzie' has four pop type safety valves on the top of the firebox, and they blow off in a form of pattern. All four valves blowing off at 250 lb pressure. As a rule when the pressure is around 225 lb the first valve opens, and instead of a violent emission of steam there is a steady release which does not in fact make much difference to the

steam pressure. A further valve opens at around 235 lb also giving a steady release. At 245 lb the third valve opens which gives off a more distinct release. At 250 lb the fourth and final valve opens which gives a distinct emission, the fourth valve blowing does make a difference to the pressure and very soon this valve closes, as does the third valve, leaving the first two simmering. If one got a 'Lizzie' with a very weak first safety valve it could be a nuisance, as it could be continually blowing anywhere between 180 lb and 225 lb pressure. This was an obvious defect and should be 'booked' when the loco is taken in the shed. None of this trouble with No 46246. She simmered at 250 lb, and lost very little steam in the process.

Passing Milnthorpe the cut-off was still 15% and we were now on

the lower climb of Grayrigg. I advanced it to around 20% and even at this small cut-off, four distinct beats could be heard. I advanced the cut-off to 25% at Oxenholme and that sufficed for breasting Grayrigg. We had a clear run through Low Gill and got a tank full of water at Dillicar troughs, and now for Shap, five miles at one in seventy five. Rushing through Tebay I opened the regulator fully, and leaving the cut-off at 25% we tackled Shap itself. As I said *City of Manchester* was one of the best and I had to make no adjustments whatsoever to the regulator cut-off. We breasted the summit in grand style, of course ten coaches was only half a train for a 'Lizzie' and the trip was what my mate called a 'ride out'.

On the descent from the summit to Carlisle, the main thing on this

The up 'The Caledonian' in charge of No 46242 *City of Glasgow* running past Kingmoor M.P.D. Carlisle on 21/7/59.
Photo by Douglas Doherty.

trip was to keep within the speed restrictions (No trying for the 100 m.p.h. this time) as we were in advance of time. Arriving at Carlisle we were relieved by a set of Glasgow men who were rostered to take the train forward, my mate and myself retiring to the Railway Hostel at Upperby. Once again haricot beans for veg.

I had an amazing experience with *City of Manchester* much later. We had a job at Crewe which we called the Chester/London. We got the loco ready at Crewe North, worked a local passenger to Chester, put the train away, turned the loco at Chester, and awaited a train from Holyhead. We backed on at Chester and worked it through to Euston, booking off and returning the next day. This job was not necessarily a 'Lizzie' diagram, but at times a 4–6–2 was provided, and on this particular day I had *City of Manchester*. We

had been to Chester and were on our way to London and as we were approaching Atherstone the distant was on. I brought my train under control, prepared to stop at the outer home. Approaching it, it came off and I could see a red flag in the signal box, held by the signalman or 'Bobby' as they are called. Duly stopping at it he informed me that there were some cows on the line between there and the next box and I was to proceed with caution. We proceeded as instructed and came across the offending animal. Its legs were in the four foot on our line, the Up fast, and its rear quarters were in the Up slow, successfully blocking both fast and slow lines. I took my train as near to it as I dared, but it didn't budge. I opened the cylinder cocks and blew a cloud of steam at it, all I got in return was a cold calculating stare from the animal and a loud distinct 'moo'. By now

several passengers had got their heads out and were quite amused at the proceedings. Seeing that it was stalemate, my mate got off the engine complete with coal pick. He walked up to the cow shouting and waving his arms and brandishing the coal pick. Obviously the cow had no respect for the Railway, least of all my mate with a coal pick, and she took rather a dim view of it. With another loud 'moo' she lowered her head and charged my mate. Now my mate was no coward but he took a dim view of a cow coming at him, so on the Up slow at Ashby Junction they had a set to and both animal and man disappeared down out of sight over the embankment. I'm not quite sure who was chasing who, but after five anxious minutes or so my mate appeared triumphant over the top of the embankment with a loud cheer from several of our passengers. When he was aboard we departed, leaving one disillusioned cow.

On arrival at Euston there were several of our passengers who gave us amused looks and remarks. One gentleman said to my mate "I'm a television producer and I produce 'Rawhide' (A.T.V. show of the period) if you ever want a job as a cowboy, come and see me." What my mate said in reply is unprintable. For quite some time after he was known as 'Rawhide'.

From this period onwards I had several 'Lizzies' on all types of trains, even fast fitted freights as by now the Stanier Pacifics were being replaced on London diagrams by 2,000 H.P. diesels, and were doing most of their work up North.

The last 'Lizzie' I had on an express train to London was No 46251 *City of Nottingham*. I was booked on one Sunday for special duty, to work a train from Shrewsbury to Paddington via the Great Western main line. Till the time of booking on I knew nothing except that I was rostered L.E. to Salop, and to work to Paddington. I duly presented myself at the required time and to my pleasure I found out that the train concerned was a Locomotive Club of Great Britain return rail tour, and they had requested a 'Duchess' class of loco on their return to London. They also requested an LMR crew, and seeing that I knew the road from Shrewsbury as far as Birmingham, Snow Hill, I was chosen for the job. I was also pleased to find out that my fireman was the one who had been nicknamed 'Rawhide', J. Metcalfe, who is now no longer on BR.

I got my timings out, wired a pilotman from Birmingham Snow Hill, and enquired as to my loco. On being told No 46251, I thought 'Blimey' a 'Lizzie' up the Western, this will put the cat among the pigeons, shades of 1948 loco trials and all that. Anyway a 'Lizzie' we

got and I was determined to give a good account of myself and the engine. The loco had been specially cleaned for the job and had been all prepared when we arrived. All my fireman and myself had to do was make sure that the fire irons were intact and that everything was in ship shape order, as we didn't want anything to go wrong on this trip.

In due course we arrived at the North Shed disc, and gave off shed, "L.E. Salop for 1 × 93 (our reporting number) spotters special Shrewsbury to Paddington". As it was Sunday there was little or no delay departing from the shed or arriving at Shrewsbury. We gave our steed a bit of a run between Crewe and Salop and found she ran perfectly, no blows, no nothing, and we looked forward to a good trip. At Shrewsbury we did not go on the shed but stood in a siding adjacent to Coleham signal box (like the signal box, the siding has gone too) and awaited the arrival from Bristol of train 1 × 93. It duly arrived twenty-one minutes late with No 7025 *Sudeley Castle*' at its head, resplendent in GW green with the copper and brass gleaming in the afternoon sun.

After No 7025 departed on to Coleham shed for a well earned rest, we backed on to our very modest train of nine coaches, 290 tons, with No 46251 *City of Nottingham* determined if possible to make up the lost time of twenty one minutes. When the LCGB headboard had been fixed to the smokebox and photographs taken, the passengers were finally persuaded to get aboard and we were off.

The following is an extract from the report of the rail tour, organised by the LCGB 21 June 1964.

"At Shrewsbury our motive power was changed to No 46251 *City of Nottingham* which had been turned out in excellent con-

dition. A few more minutes were lost waiting for the York/Bristol express to clear from Shrewsbury station, and then our route swung sharply towards Wellington. With a light load of 290 tons, No 46251 showed her speed, and despite slowing for Wellington (40 m.p.h.), reeled off the twenty miles from Shrewsbury (Abbey foregate box) to Cosford, where a stop for photographs were made, in as many minutes, with a minimum of 62 m.p.h. at Hollinswood summit, and a maximum of 89 m.p.h. for a short while, another stop was made at Wolverhampton (for water) then another sharp sprint was made to Snow Hill, where P.W. work, wrong road running, etc., caused a loss of a further fifteen minutes. More excellent work was done between Birmingham and Banbury, but any gains were lost through signal checks, speed restrictions and finally an unscheduled stop at Banbury to set down an injured person for an ambulance to convey him to hospital.

The final sixty seven and a half miles from Banbury to Paddington were to be almost free from delays however, and No 46251 crew (Driver Johnson and Fireman Metcalfe of Crewe North) were obviously determined to do their utmost to show their locomotive's capabilities, to such good effect that having left Banbury fifty-one minutes late, Ashendon Junction (23 miles) was passed in 22 minutes (scheduled 34 minutes), Princess Risborough (33 miles) in 30 minutes (scheduled 45 minutes), Northholt Junction (58 miles) in 55 minutes (scheduled 74 minutes), until speed was reduced approach- Old Oak Common, and Paddington reached in 67 minutes from Banbury only 27 minutes late. The running of *City of Nottingham* undoubtedly made the day for all 270 passengers and turned a somewhat disappointing start into a memorable occasion."

I was quite proud of that trip, I did my best, and as always the loco responded. The extract made my maximum speed at 89 m.p.h., my speedo made it 98 m.p.h. I would say their reckoning was truer than my speedometer. Had I had a completely clear run from Hollinswood summit to Wolverhampton, I am confident that No 46251 would have touched a three figure maximum. As it was, there was and still is a speed restriction of 80 m.p.h. over Shifnal viaduct and still 80 m.p.h. through Cosford. I touched above 80 m.p.h. on the descent to the viaduct at Shifnal which was taken rigidly at 80 m.p.h. as I didn't think the inhabitants of this Shropshire village would have approved of *City of Nottingham* depositing itself in the main street. After Shifnal was negotiated, I drove No 46251 flat out in my effort to get a good maximum before I had to stop for Cosford, the next block, for a photography stop. As I say, I made it 98 m.p.h., the passengers made it 89 m.p.h. Had Cosford distant been off, I may have got the odd two miles per hour extra, knowing that Cosford outer home would be off, as it was I had to be prepared to stop at it. I roused the echoes as we climbed towards Albrighton and Codsall waking everyone up from their Sunday evening siesta.

We picked our pilot up at Wolverhampton, and from there onwards he was in charge, I didn't touch the regulator again. I gave him tips as to how to handle his unfamiliar steed, which he likened to a 'King'. Naturally he said it wasn't as good! One cannot do any spectacular running between Wolverhampton and Birmingham as the road abounds with P.W. checks. The delay at Birmingham was for the passengers to take on board food hampers, as although a buffet car should have been in the train's composition somehow it got left behind, so

Driver Johnson in charge of No 46246 *City of Manchester* in 1959.

therefore stops had to be made to pick up the 'grub'. The passenger who got injured and had to be put off at Banbury was travelling in the first coach. He had had his head out all the way and though he wore a pair of goggles unfortunately he should have worn a crash helmet as well, as passing Fosse Way just south of Leamington Spa, a lump of coal fell from somewhere and hit him on the forehead, cutting him rather badly, hence the result. Although it was stated we still had a clear run from leaving Banbury, I beg to differ. On quite a few stations where the platform lines branch off from the through lines, we were slowed and travelled platform lines, as the signal boxes

were switched out leaving the points set, and signals off, for main to platform road. I cannot say which places these were as I have no road knowledge. I can remember drifting down through Gerrards Cross/Denham with just a whisper of steam on and 95 m.p.h. showing on the clock, the pilotman rather perturbed as the restriction was 90 m.p.h.

I shall never forget the arrival at Paddington, the platform was crowded and we were nearly blinded by the number of flash bulbs which were going off. On coming to a stand we were beseiged with enthusiasts requesting us to sign their itinerary sheets. We were handsomely rewarded for our efforts by the train organisers, and several passengers showed their gratitude by filling my mate's overall pockets with coins. Yes, it was a memorable trip, and it proved to be the last time I had a 'Lizzie' on a London bound train, or even on an express at all.

I only ever had No 46220 *Coronation*, the forerunner of the 'Duchess' class once, and it was towards the end of her days. She had been prepared and was 'all ready' to work a fitted freight to Carlisle. She was being worked back to her parent shed, 12B Upperby, for storing purposes preparatory to withdrawal. She was dirty, the boiler was covered in boiler prime, she only had one workable injector, her tubes were leaking, half the brick arch was missing and just to top it up, the coal pusher had never worked for months. In this sorry and bed-raggled state she worked her last train to Carlisle, shouting her defiance for the last time to the moorland fells around Shap. If only those hills could talk what a tale they could tell, as at some time or other every one of Stanier's Pacifics has matched its strength with the formidable gradient of Shap. Even now on a moonlit night, as for some reason or other we pause at that haven for photographers, Scout Green, I listen, and imagine I can hear a 'Lizzie' in full cry, at grips with the bank with a North bound express, but alas no, it is only a diesel.

Below No 46222 *Queen Mary* hauling the down 'The Royal Scot' near Kingmoor M.P.D., Carlisle, on 20/7/59.
Photo by Douglas Doherty.

Above No 46251 *City of Nottingham* awaiting departure from Swindon on the return R.C.T.S. 'The East Midlander' rail tour to Nottingham, 9/5/64.
Photo by Keith Pirt.

Below No 46251 *City of Nottingham* on Swindon M.P.D. on 9/5/64 waiting to return to Nottingham with the return R.C.T.S. 'The East Midlander' rail tour. Stable companion is W.R. 'Castle' class No 7022 *Hereford Castle.*
Photo by W. Potter.

The LMS Duchesses— a critical appreciation

by W. A. TUPLIN, D.Sc., F.I.Mech.E.

One can easily imagine the reaction of the average locomotive enthusiast when he first saw in the press a picture of the LMS Pacific No 6220 *Coronation*. "Oh no!" he groaned, "not another stream-liner!"

Nearly two years earlier, Gresley had brought out on the LNER the A4 streamlined Pacific and the 'Silver Jubilee' train and on a publicity-run they did some terrify-ingly high speeds at places like Hatfield and Hitchin in getting from King's Cross to Peter-borough well under the hour. And then they started running the 'Silver Jubilee' five days a week from Newcastle to King's Cross and back in four hours each way with a stop at Darlington. The trains were supposed not to run above ninety miles an hour any-where but they did now and again and everybody was delighted.

All this was fine, but why did they have to hide the engine in a tin case? When you saw the train at speed you could hardly tell whether it was being pulled by a steam locomotive or not. Stream-lined the engine might be, but an A3 Pacific would have looked better. It would have been better for shed staff too. Dreadful stories came through from men who had to go under an A4 for servicing any of the mechanism. It was as hot as hell because there was no-where for air to escape upwards. For the same reason anyone who went underneath with the usual duck-lamp had to come out pretty quick if he was not going to be gassed by the fumes from it.

The A4s did very well with the 'Silver Jubilee' but it was found that when no A4 was ready to take the train, an A3 could do the job just as well. So you could have

hoped that the LMS would try to manage some fast trains without clobbering up the engine. Why go to all the trouble of building a big new engine and then hide it from everybody?

The issue of the *Railway Gazette* for 28 May 1937 contained sec-tional drawings of No 6220 and these provided far more informa-tion about the engine than could be expected from any examination of it in service. The drawing showed that under the smooth casing was a 19 ft boiler barrel tapering out from 5 ft $8\frac{1}{2}$ in. dia-meter to 6 ft $5\frac{1}{2}$ in., just half an inch bigger than that of the Gresley Pacifics. Then followed a volu-minous wide firebox extended $3\frac{1}{2}$ ft forward to form 'a combustion chamber' and widened at the bottom to take a 50 sq. ft grate sloping downwards at about 15 degrees over the leading two-thirds of its length; it should not be too difficult to fire, apart from its sheer size.

But the grate had no rocking-bars nor drop-section and under it the ashpan was a piece of impending doom for shed-staff. It had a 2-ft high hump over a cross-member of the main frame and, below a height of four feet above the rails it was only 28 in. wide. It had no bottom-door for discharge of ash and access to its front and back dampers was hin-dered by cross-members of the main frame. It would be likely to inspire many additions to the more profane parts of the vocabul-ary of shed-staff.

The high outer parts of the ashpan were inclined at only 31 degrees to the horizontal and this was hardly enough to convince one that ash would never stick on it. Many designers were in-

adequately pessimistic on this point.

What looked like a single pull-up handle projecting vertically through the footplate worked front and back dampers simultaneously through separate linkages, al-though the drawing could be inter-preted to imply two separate handles. Fourteen cubic feet of ash would block the air inlets completely and so this engine would need clean coal if it were to run from London to Glasgow without ashpan emptying on the way.

The use of a small-wheeled truck at the back of a locomotive enables a wide fire-box to be used, but it does not necessarily leave room for a wide ashpan and so if the designer fails to appreciate the significance of this he may produce a locomotive that chokes itself with ash in a hundred miles unless it is provided with specially selected coal.

At the other end of the engine, it would be extremely difficult to get at any part of the mechanism that could not be reached through a 15-in. by 12-in. rectangular open-ing in each frame-plate im-mediately ahead of the outside cylinder. Sand-pipes with sharpish bends and nearly-horizontal lengths were not very assuring.

It was good to see that the four-valve-gear affectation of the LMS 'Princesses' had not been repeated in *Coronation*. It may have been used in the earlier class purely in acceptance of Churchward's view, 25 years earlier, that within the British loading gauge outside Walschaerts valve gear could not be made strong enough to work two valves. In *Coronation* there were two such gears outside the wheels; horizontal rocking levers

33 in. long behind the cylinders drove the inside valves through links about 53 in. long. The valves were 9 in. in diameter and the sum of lap and lead was about 1·85 in. The separate values of lap and lead could easily be altered by setting the valve-heads in different positions on the valve spindle. It was common to make adjustments of this sort and quite minute variations were sometimes imagined to have been the causes of marked variations in coal consumption.

The smokebox, 8 ft 5 in. long, was beautifully free from internal obstructions; apart from the blast-pipe, no pipe was less than 16 in. above the bottom and so the task of shovelling out the char was in one respect simple. But to get at the smokebox door, it was first necessary to swing away two hinged parts of the bulbous front of the streamlining.

The bogie was of the design used by Churchward on the Great Western. Bolsters projecting laterally from the main frame placed weight on laminated springs between double equalising beams resting on the bogie axle-boxes.

When the LMS announced that this huge Pacific was going to be allowed half an hour longer to get from Euston to Glasgow than the A4s were allowed from King's Cross to Edinburgh, railway enthusiasts were depressed. It did not suggest that the LMS had a lot of confidence in its new streamlined flyer.

It did not show much sense either when, during a press-razzle from Euston to Crewe and back on 29 June 1937, *Coronation* was driven 'all out' down Madeley bank to beat the LNE speed-record of 113 m.p.h. with no instruction for the straightest road to be made through Crewe in case the brakes could not get the train down to a safe speed before reaching the station. In fact, the brakes worked very well indeed, perhaps

better than might have been expected, but even so the run over a winding course at Crewe South onto the platform line had violent swerves. There were bruises, white faces, and broken crockery, but nobody got killed. According to one account, the engine 'was superbly handled here'. This could mean only that the driver got her into backward gear immediately after slamming the brakes full on, but no such thing was mentioned in the comments made later by R. A. Riddles who was directing operations on the footplate.

During the turn-round time at Crewe, passengers were assured that it would not happen again even though the intention was to go back to Euston at an average of 80 m.p.h. So they took their seats for the return journey not all entirely reassured, some no doubt considering the possibility of seeing next day some such newspaper headlines as 'Blue locomotive collides with red bus in Euston Road: Conductor annoyed'. But it was all right. The run into Euston was very sedate, and the stop was only half a minute too late to achieve the desired 80 m.p.h. average from Crewe.

Nevertheless, this was a good fast run although 8 coaches grossing 270 tons formed only a light load for a 108-ton Pacific with 50 sq. ft of grate area.

The reason why this article on 'Duchesses' contains so much about *Coronation* is that she and each of her nine sisters was simply an excessively draped 'Duchess'. So, although streamlining and the name concealed the fact, the first 'Duchess' was built in 1937. The first five undisguised 'Duchesses' were built in 1938 and they were perhaps the most impressive-looking locomotives ever to run in Britain. They were, in the writer's view, distinctly superior to the Gresley Pacifics in this respect because the front of the 'Duchess'

smokebox was almost in line with the leading axle, whereas the Gresley smokebox front was pushed back by about 20 in.

The contrast between the smooth casing of the *Coronation* and the Christmas-tree 'bittiness' of a 'Duchess' was most marked. The writer preferred the exposures and so did the enginemen and shed staff. They added a workman-like impression to the inherent majesty of the 'Duchesses' and no other British locomotive ever quite matched them in dignified presence.

What some may regard as a disfiguring feature of the 'Duchesses' was the casing containing steam-pipes alongside the front half of the smokebox. It was the location of the pipes there instead of inside the smokebox that caused that component to be so unusually empty. The reason for it was that as it was expected that the superheated steam would be hotter than the smokebox gases, the shorter its path inside the smokebox the better.

Some of the steam-passages were given some streamline formations in manufacture. (Build-up of carbon tended to do this automatically in any engine in service.) 'Fairings' behind the bars across the ports in the valve-chest liners facilitated the entry of steam into the cylinders, but could offer no advantage in connection with movement to exhaust which is where it might have diminished back-pressure on the pistons. No quantitative advantage was ever claimed for this 'internal streamlining'; it is unlikely that it did much harm.

A puzzling feature was the 'pocket' in the boiler lagging above each middle coupled wheel. This was to provide clearance for the inner ends of the hinged lids of the mechanical lubricators in their highest positions. In this vicinity, the filling holes for the sand-boxes were admirably accessible.

Among the not easily observable improvements over the 'Coronation' class was the provision of bottom-doors in the ashpan and a rotatable mounting for two grate-sections near the front end. These could be tilted through a right angle by applying agitated hand pressure to a lever engaged with a stub-arm in the cab, and praying or cursing according to temperament. When the drop-sections had been turned through the full range, they left two 2-ft square gaps in the grate and it was much easier to push the remains of a fire through these gaps with the aid of gravity into the ashpan than to lift them out of the fire-hole on a shovel.

There were occasional difficulties in getting a dropped grate-section back into the working position after the grate had been emptied and this could lead to sincere and strongly-expressed regret that drop-grates had ever been invented. Trouble has to be expected from even the simplest mechanism made in steel normally subjected to white heat on top and cold air below and periodically operated in showers of abrasive grit.

The tender attached to a 'Duchess' had a steam-operated pusher to give coal at the back of the tender a start on the downward slope to the front. The nominal coal-capacity of the tender was 10 tons, but 12 or 13 could be accommodated without fouling the loading gauge. In the laxity of post-war conditions, coal was not infrequently piled above the loading gauge but nobody seemed to get killed by coal knocked off by bridges and so nobody bothered.

The 16½-in. diameter chimney looked as if it might be a restriction on the power output of this magnificently large locomotive and indeed double-chimneys were soon applied to the 'Duchesses'. Test runs made with No 6234 pulling a 20-coach train of 604 tons from Crewe to Glasgow on 26 February 1939 produced the greatest drawbar power outputs (up to 2,500 D.H.P.) ever recorded in Great Britain, but they were for efforts lasting for only a minute or two. Taken in relation to grate area they represented intensity of working that was not unprecedented in this country.

On the northbound journey from Crewe, the 93.4 miles from Weaver Junction to Shap Summit were covered in 96·75 minutes at an average of 58 m.p.h. At an average of about 68 pounds of coal per minute, it was warm work for the fireman.

On the return journey, 1,900 D.H.P. was sustained for about 7 minutes after passing Motherwell. Further south, 2,000 D.H.P. was averaged for about 4 minutes in running at 71·4 m.p.h. from Plumpton to Penrith.

These figures epitomise the power-capacity of the 'Duchesses' worked hard when in good 'form' and no other of the many 'logged' performances of the engines shows any perceptible improvement on this general picture.

During World War II the LMS found need for more Pacifics and a number of new engines of the 'Coronation' class were built. The production of streamlined locomotives during war-time when high speed was prohibited seemed rather odd and some people said so. The reply was that the streamlining casings had been made before the war and that it was more economical to use them on the new engines than to allow them to remain in store. In addition more 'Duchesses' were built.

All these war-time LMS Pacifics and those built after the war (all virtually 'Duchesses') were given 'City' names.

The later 'Duchesses' had some small superficial differences from their pre-war sisters, but in the last two the rear truck and the main frame were modified in ways that left room for a better ashpan. Problems in this component would have been markedly eased by any designer who would dare to let the main frame come to an end immediately ahead of the firebox.

The streamlining was eventually removed from all the LMS Pacifics with the result that there were 38 unmistakable 'Duchesses' (Nos 6220–6257) besides the 12 'Princess'-class Pacifics and the turbine-driven Pacific No 6202.

Removal of the streamlining casing revealed a smokebox that was generally cylindrical but flattened in the upper part of the leading edge. Many of the de-frocked 'Coronations' ran with this type of smokebox for quite a long time, but they looked so disgustingly dissipated that the smokeboxes were all eventually altered to the normal fully cylindrical form.

After 1939 there was never any need for any 'Duchess' to attempt to match the power output of No 6234 during the 1939 test-runs and indeed most of the work they did was well within the capacity of engines of that size. Because of this, the work of firing a 'Duchess' could be made easy by building a mound of fire just ahead of the fire-hole deflector plate and pushing shovelfuls of coal onto the top of the mound as it burned down. The coal rolled and shuffled away from the top of the mound in all downward directions and this in conjunction with the slope of the front part of the grate and with the vibration of running, usually kept the grate covered. It was indeed possible to build a mound so big that the engine would run 50 miles without needing any more coal to be put into the firebox. All this meant was that the job was an easy one for an engine with a 50 sq. ft grate; for many post-war years many 'Duchess' jobs were of that character.

During World War II and for some time after it top speeds were limited to 60 m.p.h. on British railways. The limit was raised bit by bit, and place by place as the years went by, but no need ever arose for 'Duchesses' to exceed 90 and they rarely did so in ordinary service. If such a need had arisen, there would have been a case for bringing back the streamlining that started with No 6220 because the power dissipated by air resistance at the front of a locomotive rises rapidly with speed and over 80 m.p.h. or so it is beginning to become noticeable.

, Much of the work done by the 'Duchesses' was within the capacity of a 'Converted Scot' 4–6–0 except insofar as poor coal was a bigger handicap to the smaller engine on a long run. A 'Duchess' on an easy job could accept slapdash firing and so the fireman could 'put plenty on' and then sit down for half an hour or more. This facility no doubt helped in the accomplishment of an unpublished feat by the fireman of a 'Duchess' bringing a night train from Glasgow to Crewe. He noticed that his driver was behaving very queerly and was not really fit to be in charge of the engine. So, rather than create fuss and delay, the fireman did both their jobs at once for some 240 miles and took the engine to the shed at Crewe without telling anybody. This was a notable effort by a young man anxious to get back home 'right time'; no honest union-member would have missed such an opportunity of stopping the job completely.

To assist in coping with the difficulties associated with poor coal that came to be supplied to 'Duchesses' during World War II, rocking grates and bottom-door ashpans were fitted to them, but ash that stuck on the sloping sides of the ashpans caused overheating of the rocking bars with such deformation that they jammed up solid when an attempt was made to rock them.

In an attempt to follow established practice, piping was applied with the object of using water to swill ash down the slopes of the ashpan. But successful use of this artifice demands all or nothing. A small supply of water simply caked the ash more firmly than when it was dry; strong currents of water were needed to do any good. The eventual LMS solution was to provide damper-doors extending over the full length of the sidemembers of the fire-box foundation ring. With the engine stationary, these doors could be opened and the ash could be pushed down the slope by hand-held implements of appropriate shape and size.

It is important to draw attention to these doings at the dirty end of a 'Duchess', not merely to emphasise that the behaviour of a steam locomotive at the shed could be just as vital as what she did on the road, but to remind the reader of a big factor in the decision to displace steam from its position as the main tractive agent on railways. Removing ash and char from locomotives was always an unpleasant job. As engines got bigger and coal got worse, it became an intolerable job and mechanical means of easing it came too late in Britain to save the situation.

The efficiency of a 'Duchess' in deriving train-hauling energy from the chemical energy in its fuel was near to the high-class ratio of about 3 lb of coal per drawbar horse-power hour. In tests reported in a paper presented by Stanier to the Institute of Mechanical Engineers in 1941, the figure ranged between 3·03 for normal 'Coronation Scot' working ($6\frac{1}{4}$ hours between London and Glasgow with 330 tons) and 3·32 on a 232-ton train averaging 59·2 m.p.h. On the 604-ton load-test in 1939 the coal consumption was 3·12 lb per D.H.P.-hr. The locomotive had travelled over 50,000 miles since its last preceding heavy repair

and over 20,000 miles since examination of pistons and valves.

The performances of No 6236 during the locomotive exchange in 1948 were at the same level of thermal efficiency. Moreover, the engine was the only one of five classes concerned in working express passenger trains to complete all the duties assigned to it in the original schedule. Each of the other four locomotives concerned missed at least one trip for one reason or another. The only blemish on the work of No 6236 was an undue tendency for the coupled wheels to slip when pulling hard. This is almost inevitable where the ratio of nominal tractive effort to adhesion weight is high (0·26) in a locomotive with non-driving wheels behind the coupled wheels and no equalising lever between the associated springs.

The 'Duchesses' (disguised as streamlined 'Coronations') naturally found it very easy to handle the pre-war 'Coronation Scot' train of about 330 tons with $6\frac{1}{2}$ hours allowed for the $401\frac{1}{2}$ miles between London and Glasgow with an intermediate stop at Carlisle. Consideration was, however, given to the possibility of achieving that timing with a 500-ton train. For this purpose the proposal was to build 'Duchesses' extended to the 4–6–4 wheel arrangement with a 70-sq. ft grate served by a mechanical stoker of the steam-jet type in common use in America. The ash-disposal problem would have been in itself sufficiently difficult in such a locomotive without adding unnecessary ones and yet it was proposed, for no reason that was ever explained, to work the boiler at a maximum pressure of 300 p.s.i., some 50% higher than would have sufficed with 19-in. cylinders to produce the specified starting effort of 43,000 lb, and high cylinder-efficiency in all normal running conditions.

American experience showed that there would have been no

No 46238 *City of Carlisle* on Upperby M.P.D. Others in the scene from left to right are Nos 45723, 45645, 46141 and D216. 20/7/59.

Photo by Douglas Doherty.

possibility of using such a locomotive to do the specified job at a coal consumption anything like so low as 3 lb per D.H.P.-hr. The mechanical stoker was an effective means of maintaining a big fire under close control, but by its very nature it was unable to burn the very small coal that usually accompanied the 2-in. cube coal that it needed; it sent the small stuff straight into the tubes and out of the chimney. Two firemen handling selected coal on a Duchess would have been a more economical proposition.

To average 62 m.p.h. with 500 tons in normal conditions requires about 1,000 D.H.P., and this is trivial for a 50 sq. ft grate which would require feeding at about 50 lb of coal per minute. This might be increased by 25% in difficult running conditions and that could be a bit much for one man for 5 hours (between London and Carlisle). Shared between two firemen, however, it would make an easy job with a good deal to

spare for emergencies.

So the 500-ton train did not really demand anything bigger than a 'Duchess' altered at the rear end to accommodate an ashpan that would not become choked in less than 400 miles. 'Thinking big' is good publicity, but in this case thinking sensibly about the essence of the long-distance problem could have produced a more economical result.

World War II killed the $6\frac{1}{2}$ hr 500-ton train project and it was not revived after the war. If it had been, a 'Duchess' appropriately modified in detail could have coped with it. One essential would have been reliable sanding gear (and plenty of sand) so that 500 tons could be confidently taken up Shap and Beattock. The contemplated 4-6-4 would have been in equal need of this.

With over 30 'Duchesses' on the road, it would not have been too much to expect that every day half a dozen of them should be doing work worthy of their size.

That was never demanded by any regularly booked working unless, indeed, it be deemed that indifferent coal and maintenance in post-war conditions was equivalent to doubling the weight of the train.

Only the results of the tests on No 6234 in 1939 tend to persuade one that a 'Duchess' could work at such intensity of effort as was displayed on occasion by Great Western 4-cylinder 4-6-0's, converted 'Royal Scots' and Southern 'Schools'. But of course such work, sustained for any length of time, by a 'Duchess' would have been very hard on a single fireman.

None of the numerous records of the running of 'Duchesses' in service does the class any more credit than was established by No 6234 in consuming only 3·12 pounds of coal per D.H.P.-hr when producing high power in the tests in 1939 and by the stream-lined 'Duchess' No 6220 in attaining 114 m.p.h. at Casey Bridge near the bottom of Madeley bank and yet being able to stop at Crewe.